"If you want to understand modern restaurant culture, you need to read this book. Gordinier takes us into the fabulously obsessive realm of the world's most fascinating chef—and he does it with the voice of a poet. You will remember this every time you go out to eat."
—**Ruth Reichl, author of** *Save Me the Plums*

"In *Hungry*, Gordinier invokes such playful and lush prose that the scents of mole, chiles and even lingonberry juice waft off the page."
—*Time*

"A piece of writing as breathless and as urgent as its subject. Wonderful all-in, full-on storytelling. I read as I might eat a meal when I'm really, really hungry: all in one sitting."
—**Bill Buford, author of** *Heat*

"Anyone who's seen an episode of *Parts Unknown* knows what an adventure tracking down great food can be, but Jeff Gordinier knows it better than most. . . . [He] chronicles this journey with the practiced pen of a veteran journalist."
—*Entertainment Weekly*

"This wonderful book is really about the adventures of *two* men: a great chef and a great journalist. *Hungry* is a feast for the senses, filled with complex passion and joy, bursting with life. Not only did Jeff Gordinier make me want to jump on the next flight (to Mexico, Copenhagen, Sydney) in search of the perfect meal, but he also reminded me to stop and savor the ride."
—**Dani Shapiro, author of** *Inheritance*

"Follow along on an incredible journey across the globe with the world's greatest chef, described with equal parts humor and brilliance by one of the greatest food writers of our generation, as they go to enormous lengths in search of the rarest morsels of flavor in an imperfect world. In these pages, you will find that rare glimpse into the mind of a restless and enigmatic genius who has forever changed how we look at the world of fine dining."
—**Edward Lee, chef and author of** *Buttermilk Graffiti*

"In these pages, Redzepi emerges as an enigmatic and contradictory figure . . . Gordinier makes a convincing case that Redzepi's genius is irrevocably tied both to his relentless curiosity and to his compulsive need for change."
—*The New York Times Book Review*

"A remarkable portrait of Redzepi, the genius behind 'the world's best restaurant.' . . . a remarkable portrait of Gordinier, a wise and reflective digester of Redzepi's relentless creativity. Armed with a deep metaphorical gift, a gonzo enthusiasm, and a 'palate quivering like a trampoline,' Gordinier hurdles us across the globe along with Redzepi and his merry pranksters in search of, among other things, a Mexican mole sauce 'like an epic poem about history and time.' . . . A book to be cherished not just by anyone who's dreamed of eating at Noma, but by anyone who's ever had a dream."
—**Beth Ann Fennelly, author of** *Heating & Cooling: 52 Micro-Memoirs*

"A pithy, fluid, rollicking book that's somehow simultaneously visceral and cerebral, funny and heartfelt, passionate and badass, brilliant and unpretentious—Gordinier takes us along with him on a madcap global odyssey on the heels of a megalomaniacal genius of a chef as he relentlessly pushes the boundaries of food. This is a book about invention and reinvention—of food, ideas, place, and ultimately the self. It's immensely fun to read as well as profound. I loved every word."
—**Kate Christensen, author of** *The Epicure's Lament*

"For the curious culinary traveler and food-industry insider, this will become mandatory reading. With rich, compelling detail, the story traces René Redzepi's path to carving out his own radical space in modern cooking, but what's most wonderful about this book is the heartfelt parallel story—the story of Gordinier's own personal evolution, following the chef around the world and finding himself forever changed."
—**Lindsey Tramuta, journalist and author of** *The New Paris*

"A vivid picture of the complex, almost messianic 41-year-old Danish chef and the cast of eccentric, talented characters who are drawn into his world."
—**Adam Platt,** *Grub Street*

"This smorgasbord of a tale will have travelers tasting every meal with renewed appreciation."
—*National Geographic*

Included in:
The Must-Read Books of Summer 2019, *Town and Country*
Best Summer Reads of 2019, *Daily Beast*
12 Travel Books You Won't Be Able to Put Down This Summer, *National Geographic*
Our Favourite Summer Reads of 2019, *Outside*

HUNGRY

EATING, ROAD-TRIPPING AND
RISKING IT ALL WITH RENE REDZEPI,
THE GREATEST CHEF IN THE WORLD

JEFF GORDINIER

ICON

Published in the UK in 2019
by Icon Books Ltd, Omnibus Business Centre,
39–41 North Road, London N7 9DP
email: info@iconbooks.com
www.iconbooks.com

First published in the USA in 2019
by Tim Duggan Books, an imprint of Random House,
a division of Penguin Random House LLC, New York.

Sold in the UK, Europe and Asia
by Faber & Faber Ltd, Bloomsbury House,
74–77 Great Russell Street,
London WC1B 3DA or their agents

Distributed in the UK, Europe and Asia
by Grantham Book Services,
Trent Road, Grantham NG31 7XQ

Distributed in Australia and New Zealand
by Allen & Unwin Pty Ltd,
PO Box 8500, 83 Alexander Street,
Crows Nest, NSW 2065

Distributed in South Africa by
Jonathan Ball, Office B4, The District,
41 Sir Lowry Road, Woodstock 7925

Distributed in India by Penguin Books India,
7th Floor, Infinity Tower – C, DLF Cyber City,
Gurgaon 122002, Haryana

ISBN: 978-178578-585-6

Text copyright © 2019 by Jeff Gordinier

The author has asserted his moral rights

Book design by Lauren Dong
Photograph credits are on page 229.

Printed and bound in Great Britain
by Clays Ltd, Elcograf S.p.A.

In memory of Jonathan Gold,
who showed us the road
&
for Lauren,
who showed me the way home

Nel mezzo del cammin di nostra vita

mi ritrovai per una selva oscura

ché la diritta via era smarrita.

—DANTE ALIGHIERI, canto 1, *The Divine Comedy*

Dreamer,

If you are like me,

you jump anyway.

—JASON REYNOLDS, *For Every One*

Part One

PULLED UP

Mexico

I WAKE UP WITH SAND IN MY MOUTH AND A GLARE IN
my eyes. A man is speaking Spanish and waving a
flashlight. I try to remember where I am and the details
wobble into place, like a wraith making its form more visible. I hear the lapping of waves. I grope around for my
backpack and my shoes. I arise from slumber on a dark
beach in Tulum, the Mexican resort town. That body of
water a few yards away is the Caribbean.

I have been dropped here in the middle of the night
at a languorous caravansary called Nueva Vida. Unable to
locate my cabana, and unable to find anyone who could
provide me with a key to the cabana, lost in the darkness
and bereft of a phone signal and exhausted by a day that
has involved a morning flight from Mexico City to Oaxaca,
lunch in Oaxaca, the tour of a sprawling marketplace in
Oaxaca, dinner in Oaxaca, significant quantities of mezcal,
a flight from Oaxaca back to Mexico City, another flight
from Mexico City to Cancún, and then a three-hour drive
through the Yucatán Peninsula to this yoga-matted mag-
net for man-bun-and-matcha devotees, I have surrendered
to fatigue and fashioned an al fresco bed for myself in the

dunes. I am within spitting distance of a sanctuary where sea turtles clamber up on shore to lay their eggs.

The man with the flashlight turns out to be merciful—at least as soon as he realizes I am not there to interfere with the sea turtles and their ancient rituals. I pour the sand out of my shoes and grab my backpack and the man leads me to a stark white room with a sea breeze ghosting the curtains and a canopy of mosquito netting over the bed. Never has a bed looked more inviting. I climb in and try to sleep, but it's only a matter of minutes before sunlight starts asserting itself through the doorframe. The only choice I have is to greet the day.

I have landed here in Tulum because of the stubborn coaxing of a man named René Redzepi. Within the close-knit world of global gastronomy, Redzepi is a figure whose influence might be compared to that of David Bowie's in music in the 1970s, or Steve Jobs's in technology in the 1980s, or Beyoncé's now. He is the chef behind Noma, a restaurant in Copenhagen that has—for those who follow and chronicle these things—changed the way people think about food. Writers have a habit of referring to Noma as the best restaurant on earth. That may or may not make Redzepi, by hyperbolic extension, the greatest chef alive.

It is not every day that one is summoned to coffee by a cultural figure of that stature, but just such a twist of fate came to me one winter afternoon in 2014. I was working as a food writer on staff at *The New York Times* when an email arrived in my clogged in-box from Peter Tittiger, an operative at Phaidon, the publishing house that had put out Redzepi's cookbook and journal—books that were studied and parsed by chefs the way that songwriters and rock scholars had once geeked out on lyrics and liner notes. Redzepi wanted to meet me.

My inclination was to say no. I can't explain why a food writer from the *Times* would feel compelled to decline a face-to-face conversation with a man reputed to be the greatest chef alive, but the older I get, the more I find it liberating to say no. Most of the existing self-help literature seems to nudge us in that direction, doesn't it? *Learn how to say no.* But really I was just busy. There were multiple deadlines to juggle, there were staff meetings to endure, there were baseball games and piano recitals and family dinners to race home to. Some part of me thought, *God help me, this Danish guy is going to hector me for two hours about the principles of the New Nordic movement.*

The New Nordic movement was the culinary juggernaut out of Scandinavia that claimed Redzepi as its chieftain. In 2004, Redzepi and his comrades, like agents of some French surrealist collective, had released a gastronomic manifesto, outlining the rules and aspirations that would govern their cooking in the years to come. Among its objectives were "to express the purity, freshness, simplicity and ethics we wish to associate with our region," and "to promote animal welfare and a sound production process in our seas, on our farmland and in the wild." In the early phase of his kitchen career, as the journalist Tienlon Ho has written:

> *Redzepi was expected to fall in line with his mentors and cook French classics, and for a while he did. Soon, though, Redzepi had the epiphany that his food should not only be made with but entirely shaped by what he found in the forest, on the beach, and in the hands of local farmers. In practice, this meant that berries ripe for a mere two weeks a year and plucked by a Swedish farmer uninterested in selling them were more luxurious than imported caviar; he served them in a bowl with minimal adornment. He made terroir—the soil, the climate, and the land that shape the flavor of the plant and the animal that eats it—more than jargon. He made it the entire point of his cuisine.*

The impact of these ideas had escalated during half a decade, moving from the margins to a position of pulsing centrality. Pretty soon the de facto boondoggle for an

American food writer was a trip to Copenhagen to go foraging on the beach with Redzepi, nibbling inquisitively on
snatches of scurvy grass and sorrel, bellflowers and beach
mustard. "Denmark, after all, isn't Provence or Catalonia,"
Frank Bruni wrote after one such reverie on the dunes.
"For a locavore chef, in particular, it has limitations. But
Mr. Redzepi has air-dried, pickled, cured, foraged and re-
searched his way around them. He has taken what could
be a set of ankle weights and turned them into wings, his
culinary accomplishments drawing all the more regard for
the degree of geographical difficulty built into them."

Inspiring stuff. Noble stuff, especially for a planet on
the brink of ecological catastrophe caused, in part, by the
industrial rapacity built into our food supply. I just wasn't
in the mood. My marriage was falling apart. Two weeks
earlier I had moved out of the house where my two children lived. Depression rolled into my days like a toxic fog.
On a cold day in February I didn't think I had the patience
to conjure up a rictus grin of pretend curiosity while I listened to a visionary from Copenhagen prattling on about
his manifesto.

Making things even more complicated, I had sort of
made fun of Redzepi's ethos in the pages of the *Times*,
even though, up until that point, I had never spoken with
the man or eaten his food. In the winter of 2014, Noma's
influence was running rampant in New York City, with
restaurants like Aska, Acme, Atera, and Luksus promul-
gating their own interpretations of the New Nordic ideas
that were spreading outward from Copenhagen like in-
vasive scurvy grass. Nordicness was the new hotness and

that made it a ripe target for dismissal. Noma veterans
had begun colonizing the city, smoking everything with
hay and garlanding plates with kelp and edible sidewalk sprigs. The chef at Acme, Mads Refslund, had even
founded Noma with Redzepi—the two cooks had come up
together in culinary school—while the chef at Luksus, a
bearded Nova Scotian philosopher named Daniel Burns,
had been the pastry chef at Noma for a few years. Merely
having the name Noma on your résumé seemed to entice
investors to throw money at you. Everybody wanted in—
except me. Up until that winter, I had not eaten in any
of those restaurants. I didn't want to. My life was a mess.
I felt adrift and I sought comfort in hot bowls of cacio e
pepe—starch and cheese. I wanted dumplings and bibim-
bap and shawarma. What did I not want? As I wrote then,
"For months, I dodged the question. Now and then someone would tap me on the shoulder and ask for an opinion
on the latest New York restaurant that embodied the spirit
of the New Nordic movement. Had I nibbled on any lichen
lately? Had I dunked my spoon into a brimming bowl of
barley porridge speckled with globules of pig's blood, sea
buckthorn and the fermented scales of a creature found in
the deepest crevasses of a fjord? The answer was no, but I
felt too much shame to admit that."

I was reluctant to rendezvous with this Redzepi character. My state of mind made me allergic to posturing of any
sort, and I had snarked off the guy's precious movement in
the world's most influential newspaper. I braced myself for
a dressing-down akin to the notorious Ned Beatty scene in
Network. I imagined Redzepi scowling as he leaned across

some faux farmhouse picnic table at a Greenwich Village caffeine dispensary and yelling, "You have meddled with the primal forces of nature!"

Nevertheless I said yes. It was better, I figured, than milling around the office. And saying yes to the primal forces of nature, as I would come to learn during the following four years, was what René Redzepi was all about.

Suffice it to say that the man who walked through that door in downtown Manhattan was not what I had expected. Of all the gifts that human beings are born with or learn to develop, charisma has to be the most mysterious. Several things about Redzepi struck me right away: (1) His command of English was better than that of most Americans. (That singular advantage had obviously helped him in getting across his message to British and American food media. Now if you told me that he actually spoke twenty-five languages, I would not be shocked. I'm guessing he could negotiate a meal in at least seven.) (2) He seemed to be personal friends with half the chefs in New York. (3) Like me, he didn't want to talk about his movement, or any movement, or at least he appeared to have grown weary enough of the topic that there would be no Moses-on-the-mountaintop soliloquies about the soul-nurturing ecstasies of foraging while I counted the minutes until I could catch the Metro-North express back to my sad, cramped, post-separation apartment in Westchester County.

No, it turned out that Redzepi wanted to talk about tacos. This brightened my day. As a kid in Los Angeles, I had grown up on tacos. In fact, something about Redzepi struck me as temperamentally Californian. I was taken aback by this. He disarmed me with an easy laugh and a sort of barefoot-on-the-beach demeanor that seemed anti-thetical to his status as an avatar of stark Scandinavian mission statements as well as his reputation as a restless, hot-tempered taskmaster in the kitchen. As I would come to learn, Redzepi's identity as a Dane didn't conform to some Viking stereotype. Growing up in Copenhagen, he had been a migrant kid. His mother, Hanne, was a Dane who had worked cleaning houses and hospitals, but his father, Ali-Rami Redzepi, was a Muslim and ethnic Albanian from Macedonia who had sought citizenship in Denmark to get a foothold as a cabdriver and fishmonger. When Redzepi was a boy, his father had shepherded him and his twin brother to sleep by reading passages from the Koran by their bedsides. The family had endured the constant grind of bigotry from anti-immigrant Danes. Sometimes Redzepi and his brother had gone to bed hungry. The seed of the New Nordic movement could be found in his desire to *subvert* the Danish establishment, not to enshrine it. By now he came across as the food world's consummate insider, but, as so often happens, what had gotten him there was an outsider's hunger to rise up and take charge.

Anyway, Redzepi had an idea. It seemed innocuous. It seemed impossible, too, or at least unlikely to lead to anything real. The years to come would teach me that Redzepi was always dreaming up ideas. These ideas usually came across as impossible, and their very impossibility fueled him.

"We should go to Mexico," he said.

"Sure, sure . . ."

I humored the guy for a while in that coffee shop on Greenwich Street, but I never believed that Redzepi and I were destined to head south of the border, no matter how contagious his enthusiasm. I listened and let my thoughts drift. Mexico. *Right.* "Yeah, man, that would be cool." I murmured something like that—something noncommittal. I detected a rising intensity in his voice, a feverish élan that called to mind Peter O'Toole before he set out to make his sprightly slog across the desert in *Lawrence of Arabia.* Was I being summoned? Was I being inducted into a cult? Did Redzepi, his brown eyes unblinking and trained upon me, sense that my depression made me vulnerable? How was I going to break it to this Danish chef that slashed-to-the-bone media budgets meant that I might never find an editor willing to pay for this trip? Why even try?

I figured I'd just go back to the office and let this electric Kool-Aid taco quest of a whim gather dust in the cobwebbed cellar of my Gmail account. Little did I realize that Redzepi viewed the word "no" as a minor impediment—no more of an obstacle than the buzzing of a mosquito, barely worth a swat. His brain appeared to be missing synapses that would help ferry "no" to the proper cognitive checkpoints. Maybe he had an enzyme that blocked it. Later, after we met, he emailed me. He texted me. He reassured me. He kind of badgered me.

This was going to happen, he said. I just needed to get an editor on board. I needed to find a way.

———

Redzepi raised a glass of Farolito mezcal, and everyone at the table followed suit.

"Viva Mexico!" he said.

My plane had landed in Mexico City maybe an hour ago. It was a Tuesday night in May and I was here with Sean Donnola, a photographer. We weren't sure what we'd gotten ourselves into. A schedule had been emailed to us, but I figured it must be some kind of best-case-scenario itinerary—clearly it would be impossible to visit that many places and eat that many meals in the course of a few days. On the runway at the airport I'd switched on my phone and received a text from Redzepi instructing me to come straight to Pujol, which many critics considered to be the finest restaurant in Mexico City, if not the whole country. *Do we have a reservation? Will they hold our table if we're running late?* Donnola and I blearily walked into Pujol and were whisked directly to a round table where Redzepi was holding court.

The first surprise sat across from Redzepi at the table. Danny Bowien was a rising star of cooking in New York and San Francisco—born in South Korea but adopted by a white family in Oklahoma, he'd given up playing guitar in a Christian indie-rock band and forged a reputation as the chef behind Mission Chinese Food, where the specialty was psychotropic, palate-stinging Sichuan dishes that roared to your table with a wok breath that was practically nuclear. It turned out that Redzepi had become a kind of mentor to Bowien. Donnola and I had no idea that he'd be there, but for our purposes it was a nice twist. The second surprise was that Redzepi wasted no time in copping to his initial ignorance about Mexican food.

As we sat down he told me that he remembered working in the kitchen at the French Laundry, which had been the Noma of its moment in the 1990s and early 2000s—the Napa Valley atelier where the chef Thomas Keller abracadabraed California produce into a kind of Fabergé opulence. One day in 2000, a van pulled up outside. The guys in the van were selling tamales. Redzepi declined. "I was, like, 'I don't want Mexican food right now,'" he recalled with wistful regret. "I just didn't know what it was." His understanding, or lack thereof, was based on what he'd grown up encountering in Denmark. "I'll be honest with you, back then my idea of Mexican food was what we have in Europe, which is like a bastardized version of Tex-Mex. Everything's terrible. It's grease, it's fat, it's big portions. That was my impression. I didn't know what it was. I had no idea. I had no idea there was such a big Middle Eastern influence in the food. Shreds of grilled meat right off the flame. I had never heard of nixtamalization before."

Later on, after Redzepi had founded Noma, a chef named Roberto Solís came to work in the kitchen. The two men became friends, and their friendship continued even after Solís moved back to Mérida to open a restaurant called Nectar. Working night and day to make Noma into a restaurant of international significance may have been rewarding on the surface, but it began turning Redzepi into an angry husk of a human being, charred and brittle, and one day Solís offered a temporary cure: an invitation to come visit him in Mexico, eat some tacos, hang out. Redzepi, as is his style, said yes, but the trip was taxing enough to make him doubt his judgment. He caught flights from Copenhagen to Amsterdam to New York to Houston to Mérida. "It was one of those stupid trips," he said. "I was just so tired and bummed out." By the time he reached this Mayan stronghold on the Yucatán Peninsula, Redzepi was ready to pass out. But he had to eat something first.

Solís took his friend to a place called Los Taquitos de PM. The unlikeliness of this was hilarious. Los Taquitos de PM was not some delightful hideaway tucked into a cobblestoned alleyway where an *abuelita* stirred pozole in a cast-iron pot. Los Taquitos de PM was tacky as hell— *garish*—with plastic chairs and corporate cola signs and the sort of lighting that induces migraines and instant hangovers. Redzepi was about to alter the course of his life, but at the moment when he spied Los Taquitos de PM along the side of a bleakly unromantic thoroughfare, he thought he had made a mistake in hauling his ass to this part of the world.

His resistance intensified when he caught his first glimpse of the food. Solís ordered three plates of tacos al pastor. In the dish, shavings of pork, stained red after being bathed in a chili sauce with achiote and other spices, are sawed off a trompo—a spinning vertical skewer— and layered on corn tortillas with threads of pineapple on top. Lebanese immigrants helped to give birth to the dish when they brought shawarma to Mexico, which means that tacos al pastor qualify as a unique example of Mayan-

Caribbean–Middle Eastern fusion. But all you need to know is that when most lovers of Mexican food spy a trompo in the marketplace, these tacos are what they crave. Redzepi didn't. *Pineapple?* he thought. "I was so skeptical when I saw that," he said. "Like a bad pizzeria." Hunger can lead to breakthroughs, though. Redzepi pinched a taco between his fingers and took a bite. "That first mouthful. Soft. Tasty. Acidic. Spicy. It's like when you have sushi and it's great for the first time. I couldn't believe it. And my virginity was taken. In the best possible way. That was the moment."

By the time I crossed paths with him in Mexico City, his fleeting taco bliss had morphed into an obsession. Redzepi had been back to Mexico more times than he could count. He returned again and again with his family to recharge his engines and flee the pewter-skyed, bone-chilling Danish winters. "I was burned out," he'd written in his journal.

Success is a marvelous thing, but it can also be danger-ous and limiting. Suddenly we'd become a fine-dining establishment and had begun listening to questions about whether we needed real silverware, or if the wait-ers should wear suits. Like the food would improve with a bow tie. Those things had never been important to us; we'd always put all our efforts into people and creativity, not commodities. One month in Mexico and I'd realized the truth—I was scared, scared of losing the precious worldwide attention we'd stumbled into. All of us were. We were too worried about what people expected of the so-called "world's best restaurant," rather than focusing on what we expected of ourselves. We had stopped following our natural instincts and trusting that our memories are valuable enough to shape our daily lives at the restaurant. I won't let questions like that distract us anymore.

Mexico was where he could see clearly, and the complexity of Mexican cuisine—the corn, the chiles, the fruits, the edible insects, the sharp differences from region to region—haunted him like a love affair whose memory he couldn't shake. He needed to come back to these flavors.

And here at Pujol, where chef Enrique Olvera raised Mexican cuisine to a new form of edible narrative, Redzepi watched and tasted everything in a fugue state of anticipation and reaction. Of all the dishes and ingredients that captivated him, nothing in Mexico cast more of a spell than mole. What is mole? Well, maybe it's more useful to ask what mole isn't and even then you'll wind up stumped. The ingredients that merge within it represent all of the cultures that have clashed to form what Mexico is: the indigenous people who occupied the land first, the European invaders who forced their way in, the immigrants from the Middle East and Africa and Asia. Often lazily viewed by *gabachos* as simply a sauce, or a sauce made with chocolate—mole poblano, which is but one of countless strains—"mole" is ultimately a word used to link a fellowship of sauces. There are so many varieties with so many ingredients in so many household interpretations across Mexico that it's fruitless to think about tracking them

all. Studying mole is like studying the subatomic realm:
The quest goes on and on.

This multiplicity is exactly what drew Redzepi in. The
cuisine of Denmark had nothing resembling mole. He
wanted to figure out how it worked. Doing so was impossible, which was why he wanted to try. Redzepi was like
Glenn Gould going granular with Bach's counterpoint and
wondering how he could unravel its coils of DNA by slowing it down, or pulling it apart, or flattening it, or turning
it sideways. In the following three years Redzepi would return to mole with the determination of a mathematician,
the diligence of a yogi.

It turned out he had brought me here to Pujol because
he was friends with Enrique Olvera, but also because if a
person had a passion for mole, this was the place to be. Olvera's mole stood as the pièce de résistance. It was the mole
that ruled them all. It was an epic poem about history and
time. The mole at Pujol reverberated with layers of cinnamon, nutmeg, clove, allspice, star anise, almonds, pecans,
peanuts, onion, thyme, oregano, marjoram, dried chilhuacle rojo chiles, dried chilhuacle amarillo chiles, plantains
with the skin on, and heirloom tomatoes, but even that
litany of components didn't capture what it tasted like, because mole was the game that moved as you played, the answer that was always in flux, sauce as quantum physics. As
Olvera would explain it, "The recipe adapts to seasonality
and the ingredients change accordingly. It might have hazelnut or almond or macadamia or a mix of all three. The
same is true for the tomatoes, the fruits, even the chiles.

All of the ingredients, regardless of the season, are toasted in a comal, a heavy cast-iron griddle, in order to avoid the heaviness that often accompanies a mole with fried ingredients. They are then ground in a stone mill: first the fruits, then the spices, the nuts, and the chiles. The new paste is then cooked and the old mother mole is fed with it. What's truly remarkable is that it changes every day it is reheated. It can be fruit-forward and bitter or spicier and nuttier. Since the mole is an ever-changing universe in itself, we present it without animal protein and instead just with a fresh tortilla and some sesame seeds."

In other words, this was a mole so profound and delicious that Olvera and his kitchen crew did not even serve it on top of or underneath a piece of meat. They served it by itself: sauce on a plate. Imagine a French chef bringing you a plate of Dover sole meunière without the fish—simply the buttery liquid itself and a basket of bread. But beyond the surrealism of that gesture, Olvera's boundary pushing with the tradition of mole took on an extra ingredient that could be tricky and fickle: time. Instead of making a new batch of mole madre every few days, the cooks at Pujol kept adding more to the original pot. The first iteration of the mole joined the second version of the mole and then they both joined the third interpretation of the mole and on and on and on, for weeks on end, with new ingredients making their acquaintance with old ingredients and all of the old ingredients aging and deepening and acquiescing with the passing of time. The mole changed, the seasons changed, we changed, you changed—is this a restaurant dish or a passage from the Bhagavad Gita? "When I tried it the first time, I had goose bumps," Redzepi told me. By now, Olvera himself—bearded and grinning, possessed of a Lebowski-like calm as he ambled around the dining room—had sidled up to our table. "Enrique," Redzepi asked him, "how old is the mole?"

"Three hundred and seventy days," Olvera said.

"See what happens," Redzepi said.

At each place setting there was a plate and on each plate was a circular spill of mahogany sauce. Within that round splash was a smaller circle of rust-colored sauce. It looked like a work of abstract art—a study in earthen hues. "It's the eye of Sauron," Redzepi said. "There isn't a Danish designer from the fifties who wouldn't have an orgasm looking at this." You didn't want to wreck such a stunning visual, but you could not resist. Devouring it couldn't have been simpler: You grabbed the tortillas and slowly (or quickly, if you were famished) swiped the aged compound of flavors away. We ate silently, as if taking communion. "Don't be ashamed to ask for more tortillas," Redzepi said. "Everybody does it."

His mind reeled. "Guys," he said. "Let's think of what's happening here. You're taking a pancake. And you're dipping it into a sauce. If you went to Per Se and you dipped a pancake into a sauce? There's something going on here...."

By the time I joined Redzepi in Mexico, I was deep into my walking trance. There are wooded areas of Westchester

County, New York, that I now know so well, after years
spent traversing them on foot, that I can summon each
downed tree trunk in the Google Maps of my mind. What
I did as my marriage unraveled felt "healthy" only in the
sense that it involved exercise. I would walk for three or
four hours at a time. What was unhealthy was the way
that my constitutionals formed ruts in my brain, both
symbolic and actual. On these walks back and forth along
the Hudson River and through the grounds of old Gilded
Age estates and up hills into suburban neighborhoods
where all manner of Updikean mischief had gone down, I
worked over my mistakes and longings with the monotony
of a penitent monk. I gnawed on my guilt like jerky. I replayed scenes of heartbreak like an airplane movie stuck
on a loop. I replayed the look on my wife's face when I'd
told her, one night, that we would no longer sleep in the
same bed. I replayed the feeling of the tears of my children seeping through my jeans as they rested their heads
on my lap and I told them that Dad was moving out of
the house for a while. I walked north and then south, or
south and then north, pretending that I was vaporizing my
fuckups—burning them off step by step—when in fact I
was only digging them in deeper.

My strolls were getting me nowhere. If anything, they
qualified as a form of sleepwalking—like a marathon that
takes place on a Möbius strip. I have a tendency toward
obsessive behavior. That has paid dividends in my career
as a journalist—hungrily trying to learn everything about
music or food or poetry can turn even an autodidact into
an expert—but it can stymie my ability to move forward

in life. I linger, I stall. Redzepi, in contrast, was all about moving forward. When it came to escaping from ruts, the guy was Houdini. While I would nearly carve a furrow into the ground by walking the same stretch of trail for months at a time, Redzepi's neural pathways appeared to have an insatiable appetite for fresh data. For new people, too. His international network of contacts was always expanding.

You could tell when you had been chosen. Your phone would ping. The sound was like the peal of a bell. "Hey buddy," the text would say. There was something being asked of you and there was something being given. Being asked was the gift—being summoned to join the cause. Being asked meant that Redzepi had recognized some talent in you, and he sensed, maybe, that this light of yours could help illuminate the pathway forward. The club was a band of believers, sisters and brothers united in excellence—not merry pranksters, not a ragtag assemblage of misfits or whatever the going chef stereotype used to be, but a fierce, focused crew, akin to the NASA ground-control team in *Apollo 13*. If Redzepi was texting you, it meant that he thought your input was valuable. If he was texting you, it meant that *you* were valuable, or at least it felt that way.

I began to view his method as a form of Tom Sawyering. Redzepi was a tech-savvy version of the namesake character in Mark Twain's novel, somehow persuading passersby to join him in the painting of a white picket fence, pro bono, because to paint a white picket fence was to pursue a noble cause. You were beautifying the com-

munity, which meant that you were contributing your portion of spirit to the betterment of our world. In this respect
Redzepi could be both manipulative and inspiring. Anyway, it was better than going on another walk.

"Hey buddy," the text said.

So central was Redzepi's presence in the middle of the
dining room at Pujol—he occupied that cultural space in
which *his utterances mattered,* where people were perched
in anticipation of his next word—that it took me a while to
realize that Mario Batali and Ken Friedman were occupying a table at the back of the restaurant. Even though they
worked in the same business, Redzepi seemed detached
from them, cordial but aloof. A few years later, in the
midst of the cleansing fires of the #MeToo movement in
2017, Batali (the Babbo chef and Eataly entrepreneur and
orange-clogged TV ubiquity) and Friedman (the James
Beard Award–winning restaurateur behind April Bloom-
field spots like the Spotted Pig in New York and Tosca in
San Francisco) would find their careers and reputations
obliterated by accusations of sexual misconduct and all-
around piggishness. But at this moment in the spring of
2014, in Mexico City, they were still viewed as industry
leaders, and as I learned a few minutes later when I en-
deavored to have a conversation with them, they were so
bleary drunk that words tumbled out of their mouths like
buffaloes going over a cliff.

Here at Pujol, though, Batali and Friedman occupied
the margins. Redzepi was the star of the show. Around

him, like the members of Muhammad Ali's entourage in Kinshasa, hovered those for whom the ping of a text meant that they qualified as members of Redzepi's inner circle.

A NOTE ON OUR COLLECTIVE FOOD OBSESSION

Walk down the street of any city or village in the world and you will be reminded of the allure of restaurants. Listen to the conversations spilling out onto the sidewalk from bistros and bars with their windows open on a summer night. Look at the people contorting themselves in the doorways of pizzerias, staring in wonder and indecision at the illuminated menus of Chinese take-out depots. Restaurants give cities their hum. Restaurants are the ventricles through which the lifeblood of a metropolis pulses in and out.

Restaurants played this role for centuries, but they began to give off a specific sort of cultural radiance in the United States with each passing decade of the second half of the twentieth century. Lutèce and the Four Seasons, Chez Panisse and Michael's, Spago and Stars, Canlis and Chanterelle, the Mandarin and Mr. Chow, Babbo and Bouley, Citrus and Prune, Jaleo and Topolobampo, Le Bernardin and Coi, Nobu and Benu, Momofuku Noodle Bar and Torrisi Italian Specialties, JuneBaby and The Grey, Manresa and Blue Hill at Stone Barns, Alinea and Atelier Crenn, Eleven Madison Park and Estela. The menus of these restaurants probably summon up associations for you even if you never stepped through their front doors. They signify an extravagance of energy—creative people converging in a place to create something timeless even though it's intrinsically impermanent. When it comes to the ones that have closed (Lutèce in New York, Stars in San Francisco, El Bulli in Spain), you wish you could have been there. If you did happen to eat there, you wish you could go back. You can still go to many of them, and you do so with a camera phone at your fingertips, prepared to capture the vaporous sensation of having been present.

In the early years of the twenty-first century, that wave started to crest. Restaurants and the chefs who dreamed them up moved from a pleasantly diversionary position in American culture to one of urgent centrality. Suddenly chefs became far more interesting (more authentic, less manicured, more voluble, less manipulative—or so we thought) than movie stars or musicians. The rise of food television, and the way it cast a spell over a whole generation of kids, meant that there was a new wing in the pantheon of stardom. Curiously, many of the most celebrated chefs of the 2000s were born in 1977. René Redzepi, David Chang, Jeremy Charles of Raymonds in Newfoundland, Corey Lee of Benu in San Francisco—in fact, Lee and Redzepi have the same birthday. Was there something swimming around in the global water supply in the year that gave us *Star Wars* and the first Talking Heads album? Or did it come down to what was in the air—and *on* the air—in the 1990s, just as all of them lurched into adolescence and adulthood?

White Heat came out in 1990, as the decade dawned. The man behind the book was Marco Pierre White, "the tantrum-throwing enfant terrible of the London food world," as Dwight Garner would describe him, years later, in *The New York Times.* "It is relatively little known in the United States, among civilians at any rate," Garner went on. "But prominent chefs in the waves that followed, including Mario Batali and David Chang, considered it to be perhaps the most important cookbook of the modern food era. *White Heat* changed the rules of the game. It altered how chefs saw themselves." A bit more on that from Garner:

> *At the center was Mr. White himself: thin, 28 when the book was published, with unruly dark hair, penetrating eyes and veins running down his forearms that made them resemble hydraulic pork shanks.*
>
> *Before then, well-known chefs and food writers tended to be plump, jolly figures, like Russian nesting dolls: James Beard, Julia Child, A. J. Liebling. The French master Fernand Point wasn't so jolly, but he had a belly that toddled in front of him like a kettle grill. These men and women were not especially sexy beasts.*
>
> *Mr. White, on the other hand, looked as if he had been raised in the woods. He resembled Jim Morrison, Sweeney Todd and Lord Byron. He wielded a cleaver the way Bruce Lee wielded nunchucks. He seemed as if he popped supermodels into his mouth like ortolans.*

It was not difficult to ascertain why a young man in his formative years—especially one with romance or rage in his heart but not much of a promising future—might aspire to give cooking a go. Meanwhile hours and hours of programming appeared on the Food Network in the 1990s just as the alternative-rock algae bloom began to dissipate: *Molto Mario, Two Fat Ladies, Iron Chef.* If the pop-chart breakthrough of Nirvana's *Nevermind* had been a watershed moment in 1991, its echo at the end of the decade, in 2000, had to be the publication of Anthony Bourdain's *Kitchen Confidential.* It was a gonzo classic—his *Fear and Loathing in Las Vegas,* his *Down and Out in Paris and London,* but with more salmonella-laced eggs Benedict—that made kitchen life feel like a ride on board a scurvied, scurrilous pirate ship, the last leaky vessel on which a merry band of fuckups could ever expect to set sail. One day chefs were fat, crusty old Frenchmen in toques. The next day (which, of course, really amounted to a whiplash succession of years) they were auteurs, scalawags, Picasso punks, the cast of *Trainspotting,* shortening their lives with pork belly instead of smack. (It sounds fun until it dawns on you that both Anthony Bourdain and Kurt Cobain wound up taking their own lives.)

Don't make me say it.

Okay, then. The cliché no one could resist. Chefs began to be viewed as "rock stars," with the attendant celebrity status and reflexive expectation of sloppy behavior. It was a ridiculous and reductive trope except in the sense that chefs *did* begin to populate and even dominate the cultural conversation in a way that musicians had in the preceding decades. Chefs were now avatars of the counterculture, with a fuck-off, dangling-cigarette flair that had once belonged to the likes of Jimi Hendrix, Bob Dylan, and Janis Joplin.

It was a facile lens through which to see the world, and

oddly enough it made little sense when applied to Redzepi. There were only faint traces of "rock star" about him.
Tawdry tales of debauched antics did not follow around
in his wake. He didn't swagger; he didn't leer. During my
years of drifting in and out of Redzepi's orbit, I rarely saw
him take a sip of alcohol—and when he did, his enjoy-
ment seemed to peter out fast. I hate to break it to readers
who have come to these pages looking for reckless profan-
ity and mischief, but Redzepi was a devoted husband and
the father of daughters around whom he had a tendency to
melt. He did not speak in feral tones of guitar-smashing,
burn-it-all-down iconoclasm. He didn't seem to fetishize
rebellion. He was a worker. He was a builder. A perfection-
ist. A plodder and a plotter. His enemies were apathy and
laziness. Demons of some unique genus drove the man, to
be sure, but they did not belong to the class of demons that
extract payment in the form of wrecked hotel rooms and
dissolute self-sabotage. His, instead, were the demons familiar to viewers of *Citizen Kane* and *The Godfather* and
The Great Gatsby, the demons that spur certain people to
amass instead of making a mess.

Redzepi was no Sid Vicious. If we relied on the class of
1977 as our framework, I suppose we could compare him
to David Byrne of Talking Heads, a band that seemed
to expand onstage with each song in *Stop Making Sense*,
gradually gathering force into a multicultural multitude of
churning, bleeping, whirring, galloping accord.

Copenhagen was the source of that groove and you
could feel his presence all over that city if you knew where
to look. When food journalists traveled to Copenhagen to

write about Redzepi, a meal at Noma usually served as the
capper, the closing statement, but there would be a week
or so of run-up to the experience, like a scavenger hunt of
appetizers leading to the main course. Noma was the spine
of a neural network that spanned outward. You had to pay
a visit to Amass, whose chef, Noma veteran Matt Orlando,
brought a streak of citrus sunshine (Orlando had grown up
outside San Diego) to a tasting menu that rolled out with
unforced ease. (If you wanted to get up from your table
at Amass and stretch your legs, the servers invited you to
spend some time around the bonfires that they lit every
night in the garden out by the water.) You had to make a
visit to Sanchez, whose chef, Noma veteran Rosio Sánchez,
was—yes, in Denmark—cooking some of the finest tacos
and salsas to be found outside of Mexico. You knew you
were expected to pay your respects to Noma veteran Christian Puglisi—his pizza at Bæst, his wine bar called Man-
freds, his tasting menu at Relæ. You knew you'd be a fool
to skip the delicious fresh seafood at Kødbyens Fiskebar,
owned by Noma veteran Anders Selmer, one of Redzepi's
close friends. All of these people—Selmer, Sánchez, Orlando, Puglisi—were made members of the Redzepi mafia.
They were family. (For the chefs in Copenhagen who existed outside of Redzepi's solar system, or on its periphery,
this dynamic could be maddening. Because of Noma, influential food writers and editors flew into town on a regular basis, and you could trace their steps on Instagram, but
coaxing them into one of the Redzepi-unaffiliated estab-
lishments was an exercise in futility: there was NomaLand
and there was No-Man's-Land.)

NomaLand extended outward, too. NomaLand covered
the continents. Name nearly any city out loud to Redzepi
and there was a good chance he knew where you should
eat. Where you *needed* to eat. Where he knew the chef personally and he wanted you to contact him or her right away.
The importance of this was nonnegotiable. There are those
who enjoy recommending restaurants and there are those (I
count myself among them) who can be pushy about it. Redzepi pushed past pushiness to a prescriptive urgency. He
abhorred the concept of a wasted meal. (Now and then,
while I traveled through Mexico with him and his posse,
we would have no choice but to settle for a mediocre tourist
trap—we were hungry and there were no other options on
the horizon. Capitulating to this necessity seemed to bring
Redzepi to the edge of despair.) Often his recommenda-
tions were driven by his alliances, which is to say he had
friends, disciples, and deputies on every continent. The
list was long: David Chang and Danny Bowien and Wylie
Dufresne in New York, José Andrés in Washington, D.C.,
Enrique Olvera in Mexico City, Kylie Kwong in Sydney,
Jessica Koslow in Los Angeles, Daniel Patterson in San
Francisco, Blaine Wetzel on Lummi Island in the Pacific
Northwest, Massimo Bottura in Italy, Michel Troisgros in
France. Among them Redzepi was like a godfather, able to
summon his sidekicks at will.

I would meet many more people along the way, after
our feast with Enrique Olvera. A journey had just begun. I
didn't know this yet, either. The years would unfold and I
would awake to find myself in a series of unexpected situ-
ations: making tortillas with Mayan women in a Yucatán

village, bobbing in a fishing boat above the arctic circle
in Norway, harvesting watercress from a hillside next to
Bondi Beach in Sydney, tracing the neural and molecular
pathways of flavor with a pastry chef in the Bronx. I may
have said no originally, but Redzepi had a gift for bending things toward yes, and after a while I gave up trying to fight it. Pretty soon I realized that everywhere he
was going represented a crucial step forward, and there
was no point in declining to tag along. Why, after all, did
Nick Carraway keep hanging around with Jay Gatsby?
I instinctively knew that I needed to shake up my life.
Redzepi knew this, too—about himself and maybe even
about me.

   In May 2014, when we first went to Mexico, Redzepi
and his wife, Nadine Levy Redzepi, had two daughters,
Arwen and Genta. A third, to be named Ro, was due in a
few weeks. René and Nadine had just moved into a new
home. "We bought a ruin, more or less," Redzepi told me.
"It hasn't been renovated for thirty-eight years. It's a house
right next to Noma—an actual house. It takes me seven
minutes to walk to work." He had endured a hellish year
in 2013. After the rush of being named the best restaurant
in the world for three years in a row, Noma had dropped
out of the top spot after dozens of customers at Noma had
fallen ill with norovirus, a bug that sends victims into
spasms of diarrhea and vomiting in which one's guts seem
to be simultaneously melting and burning up. Even if
accidental—the virus was later traced to a bad batch of
mussels—it had been a humiliating turn. "World's top
chef eats a little crow over Noma's norovirus outbreak," as

one headline put it. If now was the time for the comeback, it would take a lot of work.

Tom Petty was right. Waiting is the hardest part.

Physically and spiritually, we're in the Oaxaca airport—Redzepi and Bowien and Donnola and myself, waiting around after a flight from Mexico City. It feels like limbo. Somebody was supposed to have picked us up, but there aren't any cars in sight. The arrivals area has the tumbleweed drift of a ghost town. The morning sun makes us wince. Redzepi points out that the day began back in Mexico City when he dropped his toothbrush into a toilet.

"Feel the difference in the air here?" Redzepi says. I notice that his rate of contentment upticks considerably each time we travel farther away from a city, but he's still in the anxiety zone. He's giving off a faint *Jesus Christ Superstar* vibe in flip-flops and a loose blue shirt. He lights a cigarette. He isn't supposed to be smoking, but he does so now and then to relieve stress. Just the occasional smoke. He'd rather not, but . . .

Bowien stands, staring at the far-off hills in a daze. "Man, it's beautiful here," he says.

We wait outside the airport for a while. Time seems to have stopped. We could hail a taxi except that we don't see any taxis and we aren't sure where we're supposed to go. A local chef named Alejandro Ruíz has been notified that we are en route, but nobody knows how to reach him. Traveling in Mexico had taught Redzepi to be more forgiving in his approach to punctuality than he normally would be back in Scandinavia. "A lot of these guys—they don't write anything down," he observes. "None of them seem to worry much."

We wait.

"Now my Danish organization is clicking in and I've got to calm down," Redzepi says, sucking harder on the cigarette.

We wait.

"Let me call Enrique because there's no one here to pick us up," he says.

While Redzepi puts a cell phone to his ear and starts trying to get a decent connection, Bowien and I fall into conversation. He, too, has found himself in a funk. After roaring out of the gate with Mission Chinese Food in New York and winning a James Beard Award as the Rising Star Chef, Bowien watched it all collapse into a heap of wreckage when his Lower East Side restaurant was found to be infested with mice and was shut down by the city's health department. When he heard the news, just a few months ago in the fall of 2013, Bowien was holed up in a hotel room in San Francisco, paralyzed by dread and embarrassment, staring up at the ceiling. When he did answer the phone, he heard a Danish accent on the other end of the line: *They're coming for you,* Redzepi told him. *They smell blood. You're hurt, you're wounded, and they're going to come for you.*

Months later, Bowien is here in white sneakers and black shorts in the drifting silence of the Oaxaca airport, another member of the Redzepi caravan who's shell-shocked and trying to figure things out. "All of a sudden you're in Oaxaca with the best chef in the world," he muses to me. "How does this happen?"

Bowien has stopped drinking alcohol and coffee. He's considering cutting out meat. Caught briefly in the Manhattan Corryvreckan of fame, his ego feasting on positive reinforcement, he found himself partying without end. He drank too much, ate too much. In his early thirties, he's already world-weary. "Being a chef, just the act of eating itself gets to be a job and it's tiring," he says. "And it's the worst thing in the world to complain about." On the phone in that hotel room in San Francisco, Redzepi told him, *Don't worry, don't listen to the bullshit. You're great, you're gonna get past this.*

"It's a testament to what a good person he is that he took the time to do that," Bowien says.

We wait some more. Redzepi hasn't found a ride. Bowien stands in the sunshine in his shorts, sniffing the Oaxacan air. He says, "I still basically don't know what I'm doing."

Finally a call comes through. "That was the chef," Redzepi says. "He thought the pickup was at nine thirty. Welcome to Mexico." Either we're an hour early or someone's an hour late. We'll learn to adjust to these rhythms.

"Are you ready for this, guys?" Redzepi asks. Into the market we go.

Shawls of glistening tripe, blood sausage glowing with ruby-black fat, tenderloins draped on a counter like a landing strip for flies, bags full of chicken hearts, the smiles of slaughtered pigs, dripping viscera left out in the open air . . . wild cherries, prickly pears, fruits with spikes, avocados whose skin you can eat, avocado leaves that smell like licorice . . . slices of coconut meat dusted with chili powder and kissed by lime, tomatoes so red they remind Redzepi of the tomatoes back in Macedonia when his father would take him back to the home country . . . a fruit called granada de moco that's split open and looks like mucus studded with crunchy seeds . . . the smell of tropical fruits and the smell of tortillas and the smell of piss and the smell of shit . . . plastic water pistols and pink stuffed toys and blessed Virgin Marys and bleeding Christs on crosses . . . herbs drying in the sun, herbs carried on heads, herbs being rubbed against a woman's leg while a preacher or a shaman murmurs a blessing—"Check it out, there's a healing ceremony going on," Redzepi says—innards sizzling in lard . . . galaxies of chiles, oceans of nuts, pyramids of palm sugar, lakes of tamarind paste . . . babies suckling on bare breasts, young women whose aprons overflow with fried and spiced grasshoppers . . . miniature green plums that look like olives, chickens spinning in front of gusts of fire while a sweet fragrance rises from burning wood chips . . . "You've seen a lot of rotisseries in your life, but this one," Redzepi says, "is the most impressive rotisserie I've ever seen."

"When a man is tired of London, he is tired of life," Samuel Johnson once said. And when a man fails to be energized and levitated by the carnival of a Mexican marketplace, he must be dead inside. To watch René Redzepi in a Mexican marketplace—in any marketplace any-

where, really, but especially in Oaxaca—is like getting a contact high from somebody else's peyote trip. Led along by Oaxaca restaurateur Alejandro Ruíz and accompanied by Danny Bowien, Redzepi murmurs and exclaims like a man in the grips of a hallucination. He darts like Bugs Bunny on a carrot bender, grazing on tacos and plums and tamarinds and fatty corozo nuts, spitting out seeds and shells as he moves. He picks up a green bouquet of leaves and gasps. "Look at the quality of this epazote," he says.

"If you have a quesadilla without this, it's like having sex with a condom," Ruíz says.

We meet two women standing next to a vat of liquid. "You have to try this," Ruíz says. The drink is tejate, a pre-Columbian elixir that is made with corn, fermented cacao, the pit of the mamey fruit, and a tree-borne flower known as rosita de cacao. Its color and consistency calls to mind a chocolate egg cream in an old New York deli. Beige froth levitates on top of the liquid like the meringue in île flottante, the French dessert. We ask for a few cups of it and chug it down. It tastes like primeval chocolate milk. "Wow, it's amazing," Bowien says. "The stuff on the top is like cream."

Redzepi's pinging around like a kid playing a video game in which new surprises keep getting projectiled in his direction.

"You smell this and you're, like, 'Come on,'" he says, grabbing a bouquet of green and burying his nose in it.

"They use the basil to clean your soul," Ruíz explains. "That's what they believe."

"Look at the tiny mangos," Redzepi goes on, delirious.

"Have you ever tried this plum?" Ruíz asks.

Redzepi spies a bubbling pan. In the middle of the hot pan is a mound of meat frying away its fat. Around the rim is a trough, a sort of moat in which bubbles a spicy black-red broth. At the taquero's elbow rises a stack of tortillas. "How many tacos can we eat?" Here is the Mexico that the global *gabachos* can't pretend to understand. Authenticity? "Nobody knows what that is," Redzepi says. "People—it's like they've been to three taquerias in Los Angeles and suddenly they're specialists. I think I'm going to buy a piñata. . . ."

"How are you gonna pack that?" Bowien says.

We take a table in an outdoor patio at Casa Oaxaca Café, one of several restaurants that Ruíz owns around town. "This is the land of corn, so you will see different ways of using corn," Ruíz says with a modesty that qualifies as an inside joke, considering the deliciousness we are about to confront. Ruíz tells us a little about himself. He grew up on a subsistence farm with chickens and pigs running around. He milked cows. He chased hens that would be killed for his mother's broth. The farm didn't make money, but the family ate well. "I was born in a village of one hundred families," he says. "I told myself if I ever go to the States, I will never go there to find a job. I will go there *on vacation*." His father almost died once in an attempt to cross the border into Texas. "Land of opportunity"— Ruíz seems gently rankled that such a phrase would be ap plied exclusively to Mexico's bloated neighbor to the north. "Here it is also possible," he says. "You have to believe in it. And you have to work for it." By now he is stout and gentrified, a barrel-chested empire builder with barely concealed appetites. But just like Redzepi, he started cooking in professional kitchens when he was fifteen.

Ruíz changes the subject. "You know what?" he says. "I'm hungry. My wife—she wouldn't let me eat for two days. I'm using you guys as an excuse." The food starts coming like an air raid. Enfrijoladas and entomatadas, chilaquiles and huevos rancheros. Redzepi downs a juice made with ginger, orange, and guava. He marvels at the yellowness of the egg yolks. When he tastes the enfrijoladas, a dish of consummate simplicity—nothing more than tortillas immersed in a bean sauce, the sauce carrying an invisible charge from a touch of avocado leaf—it's as though he's having an acid flashback. The dish tastes celestial even though it looks at first glance like a plate full of mud.

"Chef," he says to Ruíz. "Come on. You think you know what it's going to taste like. This to me is the best mouthful I've had in Mexico. I can't believe the flavor of this leaf. I'm getting chills."

"I never take pictures of food, but I have to," Bowien says.

"I can't believe this is a bean sauce!" Redzepi goes on. "You know this sauce is something that has bubbled away for half the day. It's almost as if you had a whole tasting

menu smushed into three mouthfuls, because there are so many flavors." You could not make this in Denmark. You could try but you would invariably fail. "You have to have an avocado leaf. From that little tree. On a hill. Near Oaxaca."

Sitting at the head of the table, Ruíz observes all this with quiet, avuncular satisfaction. The complexity of Mexican cuisine comes as no surprise to him, of course.

"Something is going on," Redzepi says. By this, I am coming to learn, he means that something is going on in his head. Something is going on in the sense that his reaction to the food is verging on the out-of-body.

Ruíz smiles indulgently. "Sí, sí," he says, "something is going on. It has always been here. It's the way we've been eating all our lives."

Bowien is paying close attention. Up in New York, he recently—rashly, it seems—opened a Mexican restaurant called Mission Cantina. Reviews have not been charitable. Pete Wells of *The New York Times* gave it one star out of four, describing the place as "curiously unsatisfying" and "a book of wet matches from a chef who can make sparks shoot from his fingertips."

Here in Oaxaca, confronted with the truth and beauty of the cooking, Bowien seems to gulp down the bitter realization that he's nothing more than an amateur when it comes to masa and salsas.

"Chefs like you grew up making this, so it's in your blood," he confesses to Ruíz. "To me it's a challenge to get the balance." Bowien grabs a tortilla and bites into it, closing his eyes in an expression of both delight and shame.

"My tortillas now . . ." He trails off. They're dry. They fall apart. "I'm not adding fat. Maybe I need to add fat."

"I would say it's the quality of the corn," Ruíz says.

"That's my problem," Bowien says. "I was using American corn."

"Later on we'll try making one together," Ruíz says.

After breakfast Ruíz leads Redzepi and Bowien over to a comal, which looks as though it has been caked with chalk, to try their hands at making tortillas. It does not go well.

"Why is it always women making tortillas?" Redzepi asks.

"A man cannot make tortillas," Ruíz answers. "It is a cultural thing. There are still villages where men do not even enter the kitchen."

This could be seen as both a lesson and a warning. Ruíz and the women who oversee the comal politely manage not to laugh as the masa dough sticks to the fingertips and palms of the two visitors. On the hot surface their tortillas are too thin, too thick, too sticky, dead on arrival.

"If it doesn't puff, it's not a real tortilla," Bowien says.

"If it doesn't puff, you're a gringo," Redzepi says.

"I'm going to embarrass myself right now."

"Be gentle with it . . ."

"I know," Bowien says. "It's hard."

Redzepi mumbles something about a clueless European trying to master something that Mexicans have been doing for centuries.

"But you guys are more sophisticated, no?" Ruíz says slyly.

———

Redzepi and Bowien stroll around the streets of Oaxaca, dipping now and then into hidden nooks where the decor looks like a pinball machine designed by Chris Ofili.

"Imagine if we were here for longer," Redzepi says. "How much more we'd have in our hands . . ."

Bowien nods, but he's got demands back at home in New York. He and his wife, Youngmi Mayer, have a newborn son named Mino; they're still in Mexico City.

"See if you can get to Tulum by three," Redzepi tells him. "You'll have a swim in the Caribbean Sea. That's better than fifteen thousand Xanax."

This time away is good for both of them, and they know it. The challenges at Mission Cantina and Mission Chinese Food have made Bowien reevaluate everything he is doing, and for Redzepi last year brought Noma the norovirus and the hard fall from grace. "The negative spiral was complete then," Redzepi says. "It made me so angry. It was like a bombardment. It was, like, 'When are we gonna have good news out of Noma?' You think we are celebrated as heroes back home? It's not like that at all."

In the kitchen, in interviews, Redzepi wasn't inclined to hide his anger. He poured his fury into the cooking. He coached his kitchen to cook from the standpoint of focused rage. That's what he called it: *cooking angry*.

"It was like a hunger," Bowien says.

"It was a positive anger," Redzepi agrees. (He knew firsthand what negative anger looked like. It looked like the time years back, as legend had it, when he had marched every single member of Noma's team out of the kitchen en masse, lined them up outside, and screamed "Fuck you!" into each individual's face like some kind of deranged drill sergeant.)

Whatever it was, it worked. Just weeks ago, in April, Noma regained its crown at the annual 50 Best Restaurants gathering. Bowien watched the broadcast as it was livestreamed.

"You looked insanely surprised," he says.

"Insanely surprised," Redzepi says. "This year. We were, like, 'No way, this is not happening.' It wasn't so much being number one. It was 2013—that was a very tough year for the team. On the outside we couldn't say we had a tough year . . ."

Bowien says, "But inside . . ."

Vindication.

"All these people come out of the woodwork," Redzepi says. " 'I know we haven't talked in two years, but can we have a table?' Anyway, I don't at all think we're number one. I don't think the best restaurant in the world exists."

"I do," Bowien says, "and I think it's Noma."

"Anyway, it fired us up. We got angry. And the team got closer."

By now we're on the rooftop of Casa Oaxaca. Ruíz and his crew have laid out a spread of fresh fruits and tortillas with salsas.

"That's the best salsa I've ever had," Bowien says. "I'm very relaxed."

"Are you sure you don't want to change your plane ticket?" Ruíz asks him.

"This has been so cleansing for me, this day," Bowien says. He muses aloud on how he went through the phase of partying too much, letting his ego lap up the praise. "All the while my restaurant was crumbling, because I wasn't paying attention to what got me there in the first place." He looks as though he might cry. "I took a step back and I just grew up."

"You know, Chef, nothing is life or death," Redzepi says.

"Best of the year in *The New York Times*—and then the next year to have the rug pulled out from under you."

"You walk into the forest and you get a cut and the wolves smell the blood."

"It sucked," Bowien says.

"Don't ever try to control a disaster," Redzepi says. "You can't control it."

Speaking of control, I'm wondering about our flight out of Oaxaca. The hour is getting late, but no one seems to be saying anything about luggage or a ride to the airport. We're still on the rooftop at Casa Oaxaca, sipping mezcal, scarfing chips, watching the sun go down over the cathedral across the road. Time does seem to slow to a crawl here in the purple of a Oaxacan twilight, but . . . aren't we going to miss our connections? Don't we have a flight back to Mexico City at 5 or 6 P.M., and isn't it 5 or 6 P.M. already, and don't we then have to fly from Mexico City to Cancún and drive for hours through the jungle to Tulum? Am I the only one getting antsy about this? Is everyone in a trance?

———

Hours later, sweating and bleary, I crawl out of my mosquito-netted bed at Nueva Vida. *New Life*—could a journalistic way station have a more perfect name? I am tired, and the mezcal and fatigue seem to have given my brain's internal wiring a sour coating of rust, and yet for the first time in weeks I feel energized by a sense of possibility. The Noma playlist teems with nourishments that many of us didn't even know we could eat: musk ox and milk skin, sea buckthorn and beach mustard, bulrushes and birch sorbet, ramson leaves and rowan shoots, Cladonia lichen and Icelandic dulse, pig's blood and ants and hay. Somehow Redzepi zeroes in on the peak deliciousness of his foraged, fermented, smoked, and salvaged ingredients, and, perhaps even more surprisingly, he makes you want to pick them up with your fingers and place them on your tongue. He comes across as a man with a mission, and his overriding sales pitch might boil down to this: Take another look. There is so much to eat.

This habit of mind of his—this insatiable appetite for new sights, scents, flavors, conversations—can't help but rub off on anyone who wanders into his orbit, and that's especially true here in Mexico. Traveling alone, I might be content to lounge around on a hammock reading a book until dinnertime. But Redzepi doesn't let me stay idle. He's got plans. When I eventually drift along the beach to La Zebra, the beachside inn that has become the equivalent of his country cottage in Tulum, I find him conked out on a lounge chair by the waves. He's wearing a red bathing suit and his torso already looks sunburned enough to match its hue. "It was worth it," he says. "I slept well. I was in a happy place."

He points at the water. "You have to jump in the Caribbean," he tells me. "I'm going to force you in."

It was on a beach very different from this one that Redzepi experienced one of his signature breakthroughs as a chef. He was walking along the shore in Denmark and he spied some arrowgrass. Being who he is, he put the plant into his mouth. He chewed it. It tasted like coriander. His mind reeled with thoughts about how he could use this overlooked beach weed to flavor dishes at Noma. "That was a real epiphany," he tells me. "First thing is I want to show this to the team. 'It's a native plant: you've probably stepped on it on the beach a hundred times.' And they go, 'Ahhhhh.' The world is bigger than they thought." (When the decomposed remains of the Egtved Girl, a young woman who had died in the Bronze Age, were found in Denmark in 1921 inside a coffin fashioned from a tree trunk, she had beside her a bouquet of yarrow as well as "a bucket of beer made of wheat, honey, bog-myrtle, and cowberries," according to one report. This suggests that when it comes to Noma and its approach to foraging and fermenting, the Egtved Girl may have scooped René Redzepi by a few millennia.)

Now, he tells me as we sit here a few yards from the sea, he's mapping out some new directions. I can't figure out what he's alluding to, but the coming years will reveal that the push and pull of Redzepi's early years at Noma have been a mere prelude to the risks and changes he has in store.

"I'm very inspired by moles," he says. "There can't only exist moles from Mexico—I'm sure of that."

Meaning what? That there could be Danish versions of mole?

"Maybe there is something. I've just got to figure out what it is. Finding new flavors—that excites me tremendously."

He's proud of the way Noma bounced back from adversity in the previous year. "We definitely reached a new level in 2013. We opened a door to a new world. New creativity. New confidence. I guess sometimes it's good to have a chip on your shoulder." Sometimes it's good to brush up against the possibility of losing everything. Sometimes, maybe, it's good to throw out all of the old routines and start over. Sometimes, especially for those in a walking trance, it's good to shake things up before you become complacent. "Change things. Change your routine. Don't do what you've been doing for the past five years. Read a new book," he says. "I'm just in a spot right now that's really good. I'm satisfied. It's really working. I can see the next three or four years of creativity lined up already. After that I have a big shift that I have planned at Noma. We'll see if it happens. But I have an idea."

Our next visitor materializes on the beach. His beard is thick and he wears Jesus sandals. His eyes and teeth glow with a surreal brightness. "You're like a guy who lives in the mountains somewhere in California," Redzepi says to him. Our guide's name is Eric Werner.

If Redzepi has made a habit of coming back to Mexico for inspiration and restoration each year, Werner has taken that itch a step further. He is a Yankee, orphaned as a teenager, who soured on life as a chef in New York City to such an acute degree that he and his wife, Mya Henry, transplanted their lives to Tulum. The two of them run Hartwood, a restaurant without a roof, where Werner can be found, night after night, wild-eyed and caked in sweat, roasting pork ribs and octopus tentacles over a punishing wood fire. He may've escaped the grind, but he hasn't abandoned the burn.

"When I came down here there was a void that needed to be filled in my life," Werner says. "We cook everything that's local—everything from the Mayan world. But I would never produce a Mayan cookbook, because that's theirs. I would never go out and buy their land, because that's theirs. There are many worlds that exist here. The sea. The above. The below. Pink rivers. Up near Rio los Gatos, there's a pink river and it's all full of shrimp." He talks about cenotes, the deep refreshing lakes that were formed millennia ago when an asteroid and its fracturing debris smacked down in the Yucatán, and he talks about river snails and salt flats and freshwater fountains that shoot up from the underground.

But living here is not some magic-realist daydream. Werner has suffered through typhoid and a 105-degree fever. "It almost killed me," he says. "Full-on hallucination." He finds scorpions in his shoes, and when he goes out among the trees to cut wood for the fires at Hartwood, tarantulas crawl out of the trunks and branches. He views snakes as an example of how an ecosystem can work in harmony. "You'll have one that's poisonous, and then five or ten feet away is the antidote." He believes in medicinal herbs, natural healing. When the heat overwhelms him, he'll put a pinch of Mexican oregano behind his ears. "It cools you right down," he says. Just the night before, as he was preparing for a busy night of service at Hartwood, a tabano—a vicious local horsefly—left a munch on his arm. His elbow swelled up. He sliced open a succulent and squeezed its gooey aloe right onto the bite as an ointment.

Werner comes across like John the Baptist in the wilderness, a locavore zealot, except that the divine voice comes to him on a milpa, a jungle farm, hours from Tulum, where a Mayan family grows fruits and vegetables that populate the menu at Hartwood. No pesticides are used on the farm, and no fertilizer. For a visitor from the United States, the place might not even meet the conventional expectations that come along with the word "farm."

"A lot of people think if you have a farm you have to clear all of these trees," Werner explains. "A bad farm—it's going to look like that."

It turns out that we're going to visit the milpa today—right now, in fact.

"Got my knapsack, got my machete," Werner says. "I'm all ready."

"Okay," Redzepi says. "Vamos al rancho."

As we roll out of Tulum, Werner remembers something. "Wait," he says. "Nobody's got any joints on 'em or anything? I've just gotta check." Armed police tend to be stationed here and there around the peninsula. It doesn't take much to encourage them to stop and search a vehicle, particularly one occupied by four white guys who look like they just spent the night on a beach. Pretty soon we leave the resort-hotel outskirts of Tulum and the jungle thickens. Winged insects blur by in dense multicolored blooms.

"The butterflies on this road are always so intense," Redzepi muses. "They're everywhere. It's like bug mania here. Splat splat splat splat." As he says this, Redzepi leans forward and studies the bloody, purpled smears on the windshield, and it dawns on me that he might be the only person who has ever mulled over transforming this Jackson Pollock–y roadkill into a meal. I'm not incorrect. "Scrape it off," he says. "Make a garum. Salt it. Wait for seven months. See what happens." Lately he has been reading about garums, which are pungently funky fish sauces whose roots reach all the way back to ancient Rome and Greece. "Gotta go home and try it with baby crickets," he goes on. "We have a fermentation kitchen now. In Copenhagen we just emulated a garum recipe with insects and it just fucking worked."

"I wonder if that could work with bees," says Werner, who's behind the steering wheel in the Jeep.

"With larvae it does," Redzepi says. "We're experimenting with larvae. You toast them like you would an almond. We have several recipes right now where we use larvae instead of egg. It's more umami rich—a more intense flavor. We don't tell anybody."

"The ants are our biggest problem here," Werner says. "You'll see, on the trail. Ants. Eat. Everything. It's extremely hard to farm here."

Meanwhile Redzepi's sunburn, acquired during his slacker's collapse on the lounge in front of La Zebra, has advanced into unexpected areas of agony. He carries around a plastic bag that's got the arm of an aloe plant stuffed inside it. A green-orange goo seeps from a slice in the arm: aloe vera in its pure, freshly foraged form. "Unfortunately, aloe smells very bad," Redzepi says. "It smells like sweat." In fact, the inside of the Jeep, occupied by four adult men whose pores have begun responding in kind to the sweltering humidity outside, now fills with an odor that calls to mind the bowels of the Colosseum after a gladiators' match involving gutted animals and festering wounds.

Phone service fizzles out. GPS goes kaput. If we manage to get lost now, we will be lost in radical fashion. Redzepi explains that the milpas can be identified by rudimentary, analog, and barely detectable signs. "You take the road until you see a yellow T-shirt, or take the road until you see six bottles in a tree," he says. Indeed, Werner steers off the main highway when he happens to spy a faded red gas can and an old Dos Equis box.

"You'll see monkeys back here at times," Werner says. "You'll see a jaguar."

"A jaguar is a sacred thing to see," Redzepi says.

"You hear them more than you see them," Werner says.

We leave the comforts of the pavement and switch to the rustic charms of a dirt road, which in this case is more like a slalom course through a jungle in which the trees have come alive and delight in hazing the Jeep by swatting it with their branches. The road per se is not merely bedeviled by potholes; it is more accurately described as several miles of potholes along which, at rare intervals, a plateau of road reveals itself so that everyone in the vehicle can start breathing again.

"It's like a whole new energy enters your body when you come out to these parts," Werner says. That's one way of describing it. The energy seems to be entering me through the bottom of my spine and shooting upward into my shoulders, neck, and skull each time the Jeep slams into another gouge in the roadway.

"It's going to get worse, guys, I'm sorry," Werner says. Pretty soon the Jeep is jerking back and forth as though it's caught in the jaws of a creature from *Jurassic Park*. "This is where it gets worse," he says.

"This is where it flips over," Redzepi says. He scans around, noticing the hundreds of anthills rising like miniature pyramids from the red soil. He wonders aloud whether the ants are edible.

"You don't want to get stuck," Werner says. In spite of the ordeal of this journey, he comes here regularly to join members of the family who owns the land—farmer Antonio May Balan and his wife and their ten children—to roast meat and vegetables in an oven that Werner constructed in the humid tropical stillness.

"Why build an oven in the middle of the jungle?" Redzepi asks.

"Why not?" Werner says. "This is where I want to be."

"You're crazy, right? You know that?" Redzepi says.

But Redzepi doesn't really think Werner is crazy. That's obvious as soon as we climb out of the Jeep and stretch our battered bones. Redzepi sees delicious things sprouting out of the ground like knobs, like colored buttons and baubles. Werner is right—this looks less like a farm than it does some scrubby, stumpy patch of abandoned dirt over which Willy Wonka has scattered some flora-bearing pixie dust. Mangos, plums, pineapples, chiles; orange, red, purple, green. Redzepi becomes hushed, caught in the loop of a childhood memory. "In Macedonia, where we lived, it was exactly like this," he says.

"Here, even the weeds have meanings," Werner says. "They're all used for something."

"It's kind of weird to eat a fruit that tastes cooked because it's hot from the sun," Redzepi says. "So what fertilizer are they using?"

"None," Werner says.

"It's so old school that it's becoming the new thing," Redzepi says.

"People are trying to re-create a wheel that was built

thousands of years ago," Werner says. "These guys have the answers."

Antonio May Balan emerges from his tarpaper-roofed shed and greets us in Spanish, although Mayan is the primary language that he and his wife speak. Balan nods approvingly toward the oven. Werner built the oven for Balan and his family, as a gesture of appreciation for their hard work on the milpa. "I really wanted to take care of Antonio as much as I could," Werner says in English. "He's a very beautiful man. He has a lot of stories and a lot of insight."

"That's a big oven, man," Redzepi says. "It looks like a big American car."

"You can fit two whole pigs in there, all fanned out."

Werner hands Redzepi a machete and tells him to keep it as a gift. Redzepi studies its blade and wonders how he'll get it back to Denmark on a series of planes. Balan lets us know that lunch is ready. Inside the shed he and his wife have prepared a meal of tortillas, black beans, and pork and jungle squash that have been roasted to a char over a small fire. The accompanying beverage is Coca-Cola. Redzepi sits on a stool and eats, so sweaty that his hair is matted wetly against his scalp, his sunburn glowing like pomegranate seeds.

"This is what makes you feel good. Being in a place like this," Redzepi says. "La buena vida, no?"

On the way back to Tulum, we stop the Jeep to buy fresh coconut water. It doesn't come in a bottle. It comes in coconuts

that have been chilled by the side of the road. Their furry
tops are hacked off with a machete and you slide a straw
into their cavities to draw out the tropical elixir. When we
pull into Tulum, we see him floating along the road like
a lost pilgrim— Danny Bowien, powerless to withstand
Redzepi's Svengali-like coaxings, has indeed circled back
to the Yucatán to meet up with us for dinner.

Hartwood, at night, glows in the coastal blackness.
Torches flicker. Palms sway. Orange light radiates from
the ovens. "Look at the heat in that kitchen—heat and
smoke," Redzepi says admiringly. The place has a kind of
wild, primitive elegance: If Bryan Ferry of Roxy Music
had existed back in the Stone Age, this is the brasserie he
would have dreamed up. Werner and his castaway comrades take slabs of local flesh—grouper collar, octopus,
those pork ribs swaddled in jungle honey—and furnace-
blast them to the point of tenderness and char. With each
platter that comes to the table we wilt with pleasure.

"It's insane that they built this out of nothing," Bowien
says. "That's a lizard above your head." Although we can't
imagine it yet, building something out of nothing is precisely what Redzepi has in mind for this same stretch of
Caribbean shoreline. Bowien talks about his son, Mino,
who is three months old; Bowien can't wait to give him
solid food.

"They will put anything in their mouths—a raw razor
clam that's still wriggling," Redzepi says.

Becoming a parent is leading Bowien to reevaluate everything. How he lives his life, how he runs his kitchens.
David Chang, the chef and Momofuku empire builder

who's a friend to both Redzepi and Bowien, gave Bowien some advice regarding his leadership at Mission Chinese Food. After Mission had failed city health inspections, Chang told Bowien that he had to foster a culture of accountability, cleanliness, and organization in the kitchen. " 'You've got to get tough on these guys,' " Bowien recalls Chang saying. " 'You've got to yell at people more.' "

Redzepi disagrees. "The future is not any more of that screaming," he says. "I used to be so angry in the kitchen. Insanely angry. A monster. I made a decision: 'What the

fuck am I doing?' You have to make a choice. Do you want
to go to work and be miserable? Or be happy?"

"You have to chill out or you're just going to kill yourself," Bowien says.

"One morning I woke up," Redzepi tells him, "and my
whole back was covered in shingles. I looked like a dinosaur." He had to make changes. Coming to Mexico to let
off steam is a part of that. Going home in the evening to
have dinner with his wife and children is a part of that.
Bowien listens closely and then gives the space a glance
after a period of silence.

"How hard do you think it is to score weed around
here?" he says.

We're full, we're fading fast, we're ready for our ham-
mocks, we're beyond exhausted. But Redzepi has one last
command. "One thing we have to do?" he says. "We have
to go to the beach. We have to go look at the stars now."
Moments later we're huddled silently on the shore, scan-
ning the night sky and scouting out the rim of the waves
for sea turtles. Bowien and Redzepi pass a smoke back and
forth, the leafy fragrance mingling with the sea mist. Nat-
urally, it is Redzepi who sees the racing flare that the rest
of us manage to miss. "Did you see that shooting star?" he
asks. "It was the brightest I've ever seen."

Copenhagen

Five months later

After the final no there comes a yes
And on that yes the future world depends.

—WALLACE STEVENS, "The Well Dressed Man with a Beard"

I ARRIVE EARLY. I ALWAYS ARRIVE EARLY—TO AIR-
ports, to appointments, to concerts, and then I dawdle
around pointlessly for hours. But this is ridiculous. Noma
isn't even open yet. The way Noma is set up, jutting out
onto a Copenhagen dock like the prow of a battleship, with
expansive windows that provide views of the waterway,
everyone in the kitchen can see me loitering idiotically a
few yards from the front door. I try to blend into a park
bench. Lau Richter, Noma's lanky and gentle emissary of
hospitality, comes floating out with an expression on his
face that resembles the look homeowners give to patheti-
cally costumed trick-or-treaters on Halloween. He hands
me a glass of champagne. I thank him and sip it on my
bench.

Before long, Redzepi himself, wearing a chef's apron
that calls to mind the smock of a medieval blacksmith,
leaves the kitchen and joins me at the end of the dock. I

snap a phone photo of him. We chat. He gestures toward
the water and tells me something that seems incidental,
although it will, a year later, come back to me as a scrap
of significant news. Right over there, a few yards from
Noma's ramshackle fermentation laboratories, a bridge is
being built. The bridge will connect Nyhavn, the touristy
strip whose colorful boats and building facades dominate
Instagram feeds about Copenhagen, to Christianshavn,
the tranquil, island-like neighborhood that Noma has occupied since it opened in 2003.

We wait for a while. Redzepi seems to sense, before I do,
that something's amiss.

"Where's your friend?" he asks, flashing a faint smile,
his voice a mix of bemusement and consternation.

It is at this point that I take pains to explain that Grant
Gold is not, strictly speaking, my friend. In fact, I don't
even know the guy. The person who will be joining me
for lunch at the greatest restaurant in the world is, if we're
being blunt about this, a total stranger. In the rush to
make plans to fly to Copenhagen, I could not convince any
of my friends, family members, former college professors,
or fellow poetry lovers to join me. This has given me an
instructive life lesson. For years, many of my friends have
expressed, with clarity and directness, a plea: "If somehow
you ever land a table at Noma, *please please please* let me
know. I will move mountains. I would do anything to join
you."

When I did finally land a table at Noma, everyone was
suddenly too busy. The kids had hockey games and oboe
recitals. The in-laws were visiting. It was Yom Kippur.

Money was tight. Their wives would kill them; their husbands would kill them. The hamsters had fallen ill. The weather forecast looked dicey. There was a tag sale down the street. *Sorry, I so totally wish I could, but . . .*

Because of this, I wound up inviting a random guy from the office.

Grant Gold worked with me at *The New York Times*—in what capacity I can't say for sure. Social media? Web design? Something like that. Anyway, he had heard about my golden ticket—my extra seat at the Noma smorgasbord—and having his generation's trademark obsession with all things gastronomic, Grant wanted in. He offered himself up as a blind date. I later learned that a glittering assortment of Danish scholars, poets, and runway models had been standing by to join me for the dining experience of a lifetime, but in a moment of panic, I opted for Grant.

To be fair, the guy didn't have much time to get ready. Neither of us did. During my Wanderjahr through Mexico with Redzepi and his motley entourage, it gnawed at me that his cooking remained, in my mind, no more than an abstraction. I had drooled over the cookbook photographs, but I had never eaten the food. (And by now, thanks to Redzepi's kinetic fixation on propelling himself forward, those cookbook photographs were more or less obsolete. Noma didn't serve any of that food anymore.) After the Mexico article was published, I figured our adventures had come to an end. But before long, I began to feel as though I had been inducted into a secret society.

One day I received an email letting me know that I had secured a reservation at Noma. I don't remember having asked for one. It just happened. I was as bewildered as I was excited. In my mind I made a checklist of the responsibilities that would need to be attended to: schedule adjustments so that my two kids would be cleared to stay with their mother, flights booked, hotel booked, money discovered under a mossy rock in Central Park. I would have sufficient time to plan, right? Well, no. It didn't work that way. A table had opened up. I could snatch it or I could let it go: about this, Noma's operatives were clear. The date remained fixed. Should I stay or should I go? I gnawed on this carpe diem case study for a few hours before haphazardly clicking on the Kayak website and spending—not for the last time—thousands of dollars of my own money.

Nevertheless, I had no doubt that the experience would be worth the expenditure. Evidently Grant Gold felt the same way. He bought plane tickets and booked a place to stay. Noma! L'chaim! Soon we would cross the threshold and enter the inner sanctum of global gastronomic glory. *We had a table. At the best restaurant on earth.* Our palates quivered like tiny trampolines in anticipation.

Upon arriving in Copenhagen, I spend my hours preparing as an athlete would. I check into a hotel right across the waterway from Noma. (There is no bridge yet, however, so I have a direct view but a rather circuitous walking route to the restaurant. Within a few years, the new bridge will change everything.) I take a vigorous stroll around the city and then, duly fatigued, I swaddle myself in bed on the early side, having asked for the quietest room in

the hotel so that street noise will not jar me awake in the
middle of my virginal pre-Noma slumber. I need to be on
my game. This is not a drill. The next morning, my coach,
Redzepi himself, steps in to fine-tune my training exer-
cises. The texts blurp up on my phone minutes after I have
awoken.

```
Go to Café Det Vide Hus for coffee
get the skyr and Nordic fruit
say hi to Claus
```

I follow these instructions as if my life depends on
them. I walk to a coffeehouse that resembles a divorced
bachelor's cramped apartment in the seventies. I order the
skyr and Nordic fruit. This turns out to be a bowl of plain,
thick yogurt topped like a Parisian tart with a regal red,
green, orange, and blue crown of natural sweets. The coffee is of the variety favored, as I will learn, by the culinary
cognoscenti in Copenhagen. This means that it is thin, watery, and sour—on purpose. It looks and tastes more like a
tea steeped from coffee beans than the dense, brown, milk-
frothed mud beloved by my fellow commuters back home.

Redzepi is right about the breakfast —not only its deliciousness but its proportional suitability as I psych myself
up for a lunch that I want to appreciate to the fullest, with
every molecule of my being chiming like a tuning fork.
Everything must be perfect. What is the next thing he
wants me to do? *Walk across the street.* Here are the Rosen-
borg Castle Gardens—the king's backyard, you might say.
Look for the black walnut tree. Is this some kind of test—an

initiation? Regardless of his intention, Redzepi's text directives amount to a New Nordic version of "stop and smell the roses." How often does a stroll in the park entail an examination of the foliage? How often do we get to reframe the way we see the park itself—to slip on a sort of virtual-reality headset that enables us to see that park as a garden, a farm, a wild larder stocked with food that had heretofore remained invisible? Can we actually *eat* the park?

I find the walnut tree. Or I think I do. I am not entirely sure what I am looking for. I Google "black walnut tree" and compare the Internet's images to what my eyes find in the park. From there I walk with calorie-shedding briskness to Noma, arriving early enough to embarrass myself, and I prepare for the restaurant to open—and for Grant Gold to arrive. Surely he is on his way. The great hour is upon us.

Redzepi sits with me at the edge of the water. A current of worry begins to hum, like a lost cell phone buzzing beneath a sofa cushion. Does Grant think we have a dinner reservation? I check my emails to him. No, I have been clear. A lunch reservation at 1 P.M. I have mentioned it repeatedly. With a mounting frenzy inside my skull (*everything must be perfect*), I send Grant a fresh text. No reply. I send a new email. I call his cell. No answer. Maybe he's in a cab. I mean, it is not possible that someone would manage to score the most coveted of restaurant reservations only to blow it off, right?

"Where do you think he is?" Redzepi asks me.

I cannot answer this. I can't reach the guy. I don't even know him. I send another text. I send another email.

Loathing the froggy, desperate sound of my own voice, I call and leave one of those disconsolate, withering messages that punctual people are always leaving for people who are habitually late. "Oh, hey, Grant? It's Jeff again . . ."

As I dangle in this moment of shame and confusion (*everything must be perfect, the great hour is upon us, why did I invite this person?*), I learn something about René Redzepi. We hang in the balance for a bit longer and then it becomes clear that his patience has been stretched beyond its limit.

"Let's go," he says.

It's time for lunch, I guess, and I don't intend to register a protest. We get up from our place by the water and I walk through the front door of Noma for the first time.

As I enter, I see a couple dozen faces looking right at me with the fiercely friendly, upright, eagle-eyed intensity you'd expect from a crop of West Point cadets on graduation day. (Years later, after my friend Pete Wells goes to Noma for the first time, he will describe his encounter with the Noma crew this way in *The New York Times:* "It is a little like meeting the von Trapp children.") I greet them and Redzepi lets them know that the table that has been set for two people should now be reset for only one. Poor Grant Gold.

Things move fast at Noma. You sit down and you can almost feel the motion of the bullet train gripping the rails beneath your feet. Anyone who's allergic to the stuffy, stifling languors of a tasting menu—one of those meals in which you're compelled to screw your ass to a stool for five hours of churchy rigidity, watching the clock backstroke through bottomless *Inception*-like pools of time until someone shows up by the side of the table with a single North Sea oyster that has been brushed with a froth of stinging nettles, fermented passion fruit, cod milt "snow," and eighty-day aged pigeon brains—would find unexpected relief at Noma. At Noma the dishes start getting airdropped onto your table within minutes of your having sat down, and they keep coming with the tallyho alacrity of invading paratroopers. It's never boring. You're in and out in a couple of hours. Bliss for me, but rather unfortunate for Grant Gold.

I'm going to assume you are a music fan. I'm going to guess that your connection to music was forged when you were young. A moment in solitude or a moment in a crowd, a Chopin prelude or a Cat Power ballad collapsing in on itself, high-gloss ear candy pumped out of speakers at a Saturday pool party or the swelling voices of a neighborhood choir at church on Sunday morning, the propulsive opening war chords of "Jumpin' Jack Flash" or the unfolding modal blossoms of "So What"—whatever it was, something lured you in.

If you are a certain kind of music fan, an obsessive, that initial swig led to a period of glutting, a slurping from the vat, fireworks flashing across your brain each time you made contact with the latest iteration of the greatest song ever. I'm willing to bet that these songs contributed to the formation of your identity. They became tiles in the mosaic of your self. But after a while the rush began to fade. The

years pass and you go back to old songs seeking the comfort
of recognition instead of the thrill of the unheard. You try
and fail to connect with much of the new stuff. This band
from 2014 reminds you of that band from 1994, or 1964.
This new song strikes you as little more than an abstracted
algorithmic reference to that old song. Music starts to become, in your mind, a museum of half-remembered associations. There are still many years ahead, you hope, but it
feels as though you will have to rely on music as a vehicle
for carrying you backward, not forward.

If you ask me what it was like to eat at Noma for the
first time, the best analogy I can offer is that it sent me
wheeling back to that febrile receptivity I had once felt
with music. Sure, I felt excited because here I was, I was
in. I had managed to score a table at the restaurant everyone in the world apparently wanted to eat at—there's no
way to deny the anticipatory theater of that. But in the
same way that some people get all swoony when they talk
about seeing *Hamilton* on Broadway, it turned out that the
show lived up to the hype. These dishes were like songs
you couldn't get out of your head. Maybe it was a stroke
of good fortune that Grant Gold had flaked, because his
absence allowed me to ruminate in solitude and get lost in
each bite as if I were wearing noise-canceling headphones.

Fresh berries and lemon thyme. Hip berries and wal-
nuts. Flatbread and rose petals. Turbot roe and parsley.
Burnt onion and walnut oil. Shrimp and radish. Pumpkin
and caviar.

The effect of encountering these flavors could be compared to that "secret chord" that Leonard Cohen wrote

about in "Hallelujah." We grow up eating what we eat—corn, potatoes, cheese, bread, hot dogs, peaches, strawberries, cupcakes—and develop an interior lexicon of familiar flavors. Even if you're an "adventurous" eater, wired to seek out the cuisines of regions other than the one in which you grew up—Mexico, Thailand, Tunisia, Japan, Peru—you're often making contact with traditional staples whose component parts have been canonized over the centuries. What Redzepi was serving at Noma, well, I had never eaten these combinations and preparations before. I had never imagined them. I couldn't help but think of *Le Mystère des Voix Bulgares*, an album of folk songs sung by a female vocal choir from Bulgaria, a country whose neighbors to the west are Redzepi's ancestral turf of Macedonia and Albania. The women in this brightly garbed chorus are famous for singing in microtones, which might be described as the notes *in between* the notes you already know. Instead of sounding flat or sharp, the voices of these women, rising in mesmerizing unity, can locate unfamiliar modes of harmony. It's not the conventional western euphony you hear when, say, a C note and a G note are played at the same time in a popular song or a prime example of Bach counterpoint; it's a stranger and more difficult-to-achieve accord between notes that have been melted and bent until they're several shades of blue.

The food at Noma was delicious, but not in the ways that most of us have been conditioned to understand deliciousness. You crave a pizza, a cheeseburger, a mound of mashed potatoes with butter, and there have been chefs and delivery systems that have excelled at perfecting these undeniable pleasures. But Redzepi was a chef who could get you to crave a tart filled with slivered coins of razor clam or thin raw strips of beef tartare speckled with Danish wood ants. You didn't just admire these thought experiments from afar, appreciating them as zany creative gestures. You forgot about their shock value. You desired them. You wanted to eat them again. Like earworms on the radio, they had melodies and harmonies you couldn't shake.

For me the tune I couldn't resist—my "Hey Ya!," my "Crazy in Love," my "Shattered"—was the one listed on the menu as "sea urchin and hazelnuts." The dish itself was almost as simple as the language used to describe it. Fresh tangerine-hued, tongue-like lobes of uni roe lay curled up in a bowl of pale milky liquid with beige slivers on top. The slivers were slices of raw hazelnut; the liquid had been extracted from pressed hazelnuts; a few crystals of sea salt rested here and there like flavor-enhancing Pop Rocks. That (at least to the naked eye) was the sum of it. Sea urchin with a counterpoint of . . . nuts? And then with each bite from a small wooden spoon my eyelids lowered in quiet euphoria. This dish had the deep, primal deliciousness of cultured butter spread on top of Saltines, but the butter in this case was oceanic and the crackers were earthy. I tasted just what it was and yet I tasted the microtones—the flavors in between the visible and obvious, as if tiny bridges of taste had been built between them.

In a way, the secret of the dish came down not to cooking but to shopping. The source of Redzepi's sea urchin was

a wild, unpredictable character named Roderick Sloan, a
Scotsman who lived above the arctic circle in Norway and
went diving—alone and in all seasons—for seafood of
nearly impossible purity. Hauled up from the sea in the
morning, Sloan's urchins were delivered immediately to
Noma (by boat, by plane) so that they arrived, still alive,
ready for consumption that same day. The orangey meat of
the urchin that I had slurped down with abandon? Instead
of being served from an imported tray (where it would've
sat for an incalculable amount of time), it had been scooped
out by one of the cooks at Noma seconds before it was
placed down in front of me. No, it was not a bowl of cacio e
pepe or a gooey cheeseburger, but it was probably the most
delicious thing I had ever eaten.

As for Grant Gold, he missed it. He missed the sea urchin and hazelnuts, just as he missed the lobster and nasturtium and the soft funky custard of egg yolk nestled in
a field of tiny potatoes (about the size of chickpeas) and the
essence of rose petals. He missed the lingonberry juice and
the apple-pine juice and the natural wines from producers like Christian Tschida and Bruno Schueller and Franz
Strohmeier. An exquisite meal was being served and Gold
had forked out the financial resources to have access to it,
but he was somewhere across town, asleep, having made
the fateful mistake of succumbing to jet lag, and having
(as a result) sunk into a slumber from which there was
no reviving him or retrieving him. The absence of Grant
Gold carried through my first meal at Noma like the pa-
thetically comic low note of a bassoon. Now and then I
would raise a glass of wine to the empty space at my table,

toasting the man who failed to show up at the best restaurant in the world.

And then, like Kramer bursting through the door of Jerry Seinfeld's apartment in a frantic huff, Grant Gold tragically appeared. He arrived in the foyer of Noma with a look of horror and shame on his face. He had come very late, but not too late, which almost made it worse. Ever the delicate conductors of hospitality, the Noma team restored Gold's chair next to mine, and his tableware, and granted him the dignity of enjoying three savory courses as well as pastry chef Rosio Sánchez's desserts: a giant chicharrón covered in chocolate, a buttery Danish pastry, a sort of ice cream tart made with aronia berries and the seaweed known as dulse, cold creamy quenelles that managed to match the flavors of potato and plum.

Grant Gold had missed most of the concert, but he did show up for the encore—not that that was enough to erase the glaze of embarrassment from his eyes. When the meal had ended and someone at Noma handed us our printed menus so that we would have a memento of the experience, mine listed all of the dishes that I had eaten. Gold's had a big blank space to remind him of all the dishes that he had missed.

Matthew Houck, the musician who goes by the nom de plume Phosphorescent, has a song called "C'est La Vie No. 2." It's a plaintive ballad of lost love, the "After the Gold Rush" of twenty-first-century heartbreak. Here are some lyrics:

I stood out in the night
In an empty field and I called your name
I don't stand out all night in empty fields
And call your name no more

The narrator of the song may seem to have evolved to a healthier place. He's no longer howling out a woman's name in an open field, after all. But he's still dealing with the aftermath. Old love hasn't been replaced by new love. Old love has turned him into a ghost. If he no longer haunts the moors, standing in the rain and calling out her name, he is nevertheless haunted by the memory of having done so. He does not expect to get his former life back, but he has fetishized what it felt like to lose it. He is longing for longing. Pain is preferable to numbness—*c'est la vie*.

It was a numbness I had slipped into myself. My headscape from day to day was the opposite of hunger, the antithesis of engagement: the walking trance. I interviewed people for a living yet I had less and less patience for what they wanted to tell me. When Redzepi had reached out to meet, I had come very close to saying no. Saying no increasingly felt like the only sensible response. But now I had said yes at least twice, and I was standing in the middle of Saturday Night Projects, surrounded by people whose hunger and engagement could only be described as ferocious.

Do you get tired? I mean really tired—weary from your eyes to the soles of your feet. Just . . . *spent*. That feeling of having nothing left to give, mentally or physically—that sense of seeing no other solution than to forklift your own bones into bed and mummify them in layers of blankets and sheets. Well, magnify that fatigue. Triple it. Imagine that you've been on your feet all week hustling in the kitchen at Noma. You have helped deliver dinner (and sometimes lunch, too) every day, preparing dishes of beef tartare and langoustines with a summoning of mental attention comparable to that of an opera singer or a grand master of chess. You and the rest of the team in the kitchen have been careening toward Saturday night, counting the hours as you've approached the much-needed Sunday-Monday breather, gasping for that relief like a pearl diver chasing bubbles as you return to the surface to refill your lungs. Sometimes Sunday comes and all you want to do is sleep through the day. Sometimes your body just does that.

Well, imagine reaching Saturday night—watching the last dessert of the week depart from the kitchen, hearing Lau Richter accepting the final expressions of gratitude from a few guests who seem too enchanted to leave the lounge area—and gearing up for a whole new task. Imagine you're that tired and you still have to talk yourself into cranking up the energy to cook all over again. Immediately. That's Saturday Night Projects. Because of Redzepi's devotion to the gospel of Always Moving Forward, the denizens of the Noma kitchen could not content themselves with a cold beer as midnight loomed. Instead what went down on Saturday nights—except on those rare occasions when Redzepi himself was too exhausted or when he sensed the same near-collapse among the troops—was something of a competition, a cage match, a culinary version of Mad

Max at the Thunderdome. Saturday Night Projects—the name sounds tame enough, and it's true that Redzepi was more inclined to shower compliments on his gastronomic gladiators than to cast aspersions. Nevertheless, on the nights when I was invited to stand in the kitchen and witness Saturday Night Projects, I couldn't help but think that there was something superhuman in the effort required to make it happen.

The front doors of the restaurant would close. The guests would go home—except for the few who, now and then, decided to stick around and be spectators. The lights of the dining room would dim. The countertops in the kitchen would be cleared off. Off in the margins, young cooks would have their heads lowered as they fussed over the elements of dishes that they had been dreaming up and adjusting all week long. Most of the time these were the youngest, greenest cooks in the kitchen, and because of the global nature of Redzepi's hiring practices, Saturday Night Projects would wind up looking like a weird subcategory of the Olympics: Finland versus Mexico versus Japan versus Italy versus Ecuador in a transcontinental cookoff. The athletes, as it were, had been instructed to come up with a new dish. Something to eat. Something Noma-ish but personal as well—something that, ideally, represented the essence of their own relationship with cooking as interpreted through the foraged-and-fermented filter of the Noma philosophy.

The cooks would ceremonially bring the dishes out to the counters, which were illuminated by an overhead light, even though the rest of the restaurant seemed to have gone dark. This heightened the sense that we were in an arena, and the drama would build as Noma's leaders and the spectators would crowd around the counters to get a good look at the food. The dish had to be prepared in ample quantity so that everyone attending Saturday Night Projects could dip in a spoon or a fork and get a taste—after, of course, Redzepi and his lieutenants had gone first. There wasn't a winner per se, but even a couple of sweet droplets of approval from the boss constituted a victory that could nourish a young cook during the long sleep of the two days off. "Wow! Delicious! If you had that at a Michelin-starred restaurant, the best restaurant, you wouldn't blink," Redzepi announced one night when I was there, after having tasted an unlikely number made with Danish summer tomatoes and artichokes. As Redzepi said this, I watched a weary young Italian cook fill up with fresh energy like a pitcher replenished with water. "Honestly I think it's incredibly high level."

"I didn't taste it, Chef," said someone in the crowd.

"You have to be aggressive," said head chef Dan Giusti.

Once when I was a spectator at Saturday Night Projects, I saw that Fabian von Hauske was in the crowd. A young chef who had grown up in Mexico and had, while still in his twenties, opened two successful restaurants on Manhattan's Lower East Side—Contra and Wildair—with comrade Jeremiah Stone, von Hauske counted himself as a member of the Noma diaspora. He had staged in the kitchen in Copenhagen for a few months in 2010. He had participated in Saturday Night Projects in the past; now he got to observe it. The push that Saturday Night

Projects embodied—the challenge of coming up with a new delight week after week while in the midst of doing your regular job—had become part of his culinary DNA. But he continued to marvel at how Noma insisted on reinventing itself season after season. "A different mentality" is how he described it to me. "The restaurant has changed every year. It keeps changing, which is crazy." As he and I talked, a young cook from Brazil described the dish that she had conjured for Projects. She was serving lamb liver, and when she was growing up, she said, liver would be served still warm from the body heat of the slaughtered animal that had supplied it. To replicate the spirit of that, she had given the liver a quick char over flames but left the interior more or less raw, then had dressed the organ with nasturtium flowers and an oil derived from St. John's wort.

"It's pretty daring to put up liver," Redzepi said to her after he sampled it. "I'm like you—I happened to grow up on liver and to me it's the best damn thing in the world." While he spoke, the young Brazilian chef visibly gulped. Redzepi conceded that "raw liver might scare off the in-betweeners," but, hey, the in-betweeners were not exactly Noma's target audience.

"What's next?" Redzepi asked. Next was a young cook from Ireland; she had devised a twist on Irish coffee, with a whiskey-spritzed crème anglaise and an edible soil that tasted like your morning brew. "Have you done this before?" he asked. She was a Saturday Night Projects initiate. "You've never done this before? This is the first time you've ever created a dish? Wow. That's pretty impressive." Redzepi looked to the crowd as they dug in with their spoons.

"Have you ever tasted this before? No. That's how I feel, too. I can't say that I've ever had this flavor in my mouth before. And that's always puzzling." He looked back at the cook. He had concerns about the temperature and the texture. "It's too cold," he said. "Like, *cold*. Like, hurt-your-teeth cold." I couldn't tell whether Redzepi actually *liked* the dish; nevertheless he found a way to leave its creator with a frisson of achievement. "You today have taught us something new about flavor," he told her. "You have a gift that's very rare."

When the Saturday Night Projects ended, it seemed as though no one in the kitchen was tired anymore—including me. This came as a surprise. The task of piling extra work on top of a week's worth of work appeared, paradoxically, to energize the room. It may have been more punishing in the early days of Noma, when Saturday Night Projects was not some isolated exercise. "We used to do this *every* night," Redzepi said. "Every night. And every person." As he recalled in *Journal*, his diary-like 2013 book recounting a year in the life of Noma:

> *Seven or eight years ago, on a cold winter day, I told the entire kitchen staff, much to their disbelief, that every night after service each person had to prepare something to share. It could be something simple, not necessarily a complete dish; even a better way of peeling carrots could be enough. At the time I was trying to create a team of bright chefs who were fully present and adept, but what I had for the most part were robots: human machines who'd been trained to follow a recipe as though it were*

some sort of absolute truth, forgetting the impulses and reactions that are necessary when working with something that's alive. After all, it's the chef cooking the food who makes the magic, not the recipe; a drop of acidity here or there, even when not called for in the recipe, can make all the difference. . . . Recipes should be strong guidelines, not fixed scripture.

Even when Saturday Night Projects was over, the week's work wasn't. "Let's do what we do, which is to clean up," Redzepi barked. "And then go change and you guys can have your beers." Music—mostly hip-hop and heavy metal—would flood the room and the cooks would apply themselves to soaping and scrubbing every last millimeter of the kitchen.

Giusti told me that Saturday Night Projects seemed, on the surface, like a natural source of anxiety, especially for those participants who spent a full week fretting over it. "It's always super-stressful," he said. "When they sauce the plates their hands are shaking." But its purpose was to restore the troops, not to drain or dispirit them. "We try to keep it as constructive as possible," he said. "It's not a very good exercise if people are afraid. If it's a negative experience, it's a disaster." Rarely did any of the Saturday Night Projects experiments end up as part of the Noma repertoire. (That would be sort of like the equivalent of a homemade iPhone video winning a top prize at the Sundance Film Festival.) But the exercise helped the cooks understand more about themselves and their chosen profession. And from a leadership perspective, it helped Redzepi learn more about who was working for him—their strengths, their weaknesses.

"Are you going to explain to us what's happening?" he asked a taciturn Finnish cook once at Saturday Night Projects. The dish that the Finn presented involved a fermented potato bread topped with tender tongue that had simmered for something like fifty-five hours. "That's a long time," Redzepi said. He dug in. "Taste this, guys. This is fucking amazing. How many of you love very tender tongue? Let's say you had this dish at a restaurant. Would you be happy? That's really fucking good. To me you could even just serve this bread like this and pour a sauce over it. It's amazing. I don't need those chestnuts. Four slices of bland chestnuts. What was the point of that? Why do you put something on that's not good? Just fuck it. Leave it off." The fullness of Redzepi's praise managed to vaporize any residual sting regarding those chestnuts. Fuck it. Leave it off. Yes, Chef.

After my meal without Grant Gold, I lingered in the Noma kitchen for a while, learning about the team's most recent experiments with fermentation and gearing up to witness Saturday Night Projects for the first time. I would come to learn that there was always a strange sense of momentousness in the Noma kitchen. *Everything* seemed to *matter.* If a hungover cook at Noma ever felt like phoning it in some afternoon, he or she would have to be crafty about disguising his or her lethargy. There was always news as well. The news during that visit was that Rosio Sánchez, Noma's pastry chef and a crucial member of the R&D pod, would soon be parting ways with Noma so that she could open a taco stand in Copenhagen. Who would replace her?

I asked a few times and no one would tell me. So I decided to hazard a guess. My guess was correct, as Giusti confirmed to me with a nod: Noma was about to bring in a new pastry chef, an American, who had grown up in the unlikely training ground of the Bronx.

Macedonia

Also known as the Republic of
North Macedonia,
not to be confused with the region of Greece
also called Macedonia

A POT OF BEANS, SIMMERING ON A STOVE.

The recipe is simple. Soak the beans overnight to tenderize them. Heat them in chicken broth and just leave them there on a low flame for a couple of hours. You should have about four times more broth than beans. Throw in a few peeled cloves of garlic. Some sweet tomatoes. "So here comes the secret part," as Nadine Levy Redzepi can tell you. About twenty minutes before the beans are finished, drop in three bags of chamomile tea. Yes, you're infusing the beans with the flavor of dried flowers. Leave the tea bags there for five minutes but don't let them disintegrate. You don't want herbal flotsam swilling around.

Season the beans with salt, ladle them into a bowl, crown them with fresh chopped herbs and a lizard's tail of red chili oil. Oh—and don't forget to fish out the tomato skins, at least if you happen to be making this dish for René Redzepi. Or maybe you take the extra step, in advance, of cooking the tomatoes way down. "You have to simmer the tomato sauce for a day to liquefy the skins," he'd advise you. "When I was a child, my father would do that. My mother wouldn't. For some reason the skins gross me out as a texture in a sauce."

A pot of beans simmering on a stove: as the years passed, Redzepi would find himself hungering for this, both as sustenance and as memory. Redzepi's father had eaten this dish almost every day. It had been his ritual, his consistent repast. A pot of beans. Redzepi didn't serve anything like it at Noma, but he ate it at home, this echo of life back in Macedonia—peppers and herbs and olive oil, tomatoes and garlic and the floral scent of a summer field, far away from the liver paste and pickled fish of Denmark. Redzepi would find himself returning to this dish more often as his father's body raged with cancer.

All the press about the New Nordic movement obscured a central fact: Redzepi's connection to anything Nordic was tenuous at best. He portrayed himself as more of an interloper than a native, and even though his mother came from Denmark's Protestant majority, Redzepi poked fun at Protestants any chance he got, scornful of their squeamishness, their tame palates, their historical compulsion to crush and pave over wildness. His first real gambit as a cook had arisen from his memories of Macedonia. Redzepi, at fifteen, had been more or less nudged out of high school by teachers who saw him as a dunce, and he stumbled into culinary training mostly because a friend of his was enrolling in cooking school and Redzepi figured he'd go along. The first dish he cooked there? A plate of spicy chicken and rice, with a cashew sauce, that happened to be his father's specialty from back home. After cooking school, during the decade between 1993 and 2003 (when he opened Noma), Redzepi's accidental career had become suffused with ambition. He had gathered insights along the way, working and watching in the kitchens of Le Jardin des Sens in France, El Bulli in Spain, The French Laundry in California, and Kong Hans Kælder in Copenhagen. In each place he came across as a hungry student. Whether the cuisine being served was traditional or experimental, he wanted to know everything about how it was put together. It was as though he needed to make up for lost time. In his youth he had had no exposure to deconstructed fare like that being served at chef Ferran Adrià's paradigm-shifting, smoke-foamed El Bulli. After one dinner there, Redzepi made a beeline for the kitchen and begged for a job.

By now, years later, people in the press couldn't help but focus on the "Nordic" part of the New Nordic formulation, but that word was something of a red herring, so to speak. The important word was "new." The menu at Noma represented an attempt to refashion the very concept of Scandinavian cuisine, and what that meant had as much (if not more) to do with Macedonia than with the realm of smørrebrød and flødeboller. Redzepi's approach was a way of hitting the reset button and asking, *What if we were to see this land with new eyes?* What if we were to revise it, reconsider it? What if the framework wasn't the Protestant civilization that'd been laid down like a frigid veneer but the indigenous riches that had existed before that— and that still existed all over the place, if anyone took the time to notice them? That way of thinking could be traced back to childhood idylls that Redzepi and his twin brother,

Kenneth, had spent in Macedonia, holidays that had embedded in him the same things he would later seek out and
bring to the table in Japan and Mexico and Australia: wild
nature and warm sunshine.

"For so long, many chefs in this part of the world have
regarded ingredients from southern Europe as superior,"
Redzepi once wrote in his *Journal*. "Now we realize that
our own diverse produce has value. We've come to learn
that the difference isn't in the quality of the produce, but
the cultural history of appreciating cuisine, something I
call the *Babette's Feast* Syndrome. *Babette's Feast* is a lovely
story where a female French master chef escapes war and
finds herself deep in the Protestant north of Denmark.
Here she encounters a people who only experience life
through the written word of the Bible, who block out un-
godly pleasures such as delicious food. What the fuck is
a godly pleasure anyway? The bounties of the seasons and
welcoming delicious flavours should be a part of your life,
a part of your culture."

In Macedonia, that bounty was ever-present, at least in
Redzepi's memory. "I never saw it as anything valuable
that would shape the future me," he told me, "but it really
does." When he talked about Yugoslavia in the years preceding the bloodshed of the Balkan Wars, it sounded like
Eden—no locks on the doors, kids freely darting around in
the fields, fresh vegetables eaten moments after they had
been harvested. His father, a man of Albanian ancestry,
had grown up among farmers, around animals. You'd ride
a horse to get somewhere. You'd eat dinner and then your
whole family would clear space in the dining room and lay

blankets on the floor to sleep. If you got thirsty, you had a drink made with rosewater. You went off looking for chestnuts when they were in season. There was no refrigeration in the house and everything was cooked over an open fire. Young René churned butter and milked cows. From this time in his life, the long slow summer weeks that he spent in Macedonia, Redzepi would internalize his passion for foraging, and he would also take home his father's recipe for beans simmered with tomatoes and garlic.

"Balkan dog"—that's what people would call Redzepi back in Denmark. For those who happen to notice that his kitchen at Noma was staffed with and powered by immigrants, it's useful to remember that Redzepi always viewed himself as one. He was drawn to those cooks who seemed to come from a place outside of the establishment. He knew how that felt. He knew what it was like trying to find an apartment and getting the cold shoulder because of your foreign-sounding name. When he was eleven years old, Redzepi worked as a paperboy, delivering the news on five different routes around the city. "This was about helping my mother and father pay the rent, and also about sending money back to our family in Macedonia," he would tell the *Wall Street Journal*. Immigrants from Mexico and Central America who crossed the border into the United States, looking for low-wage jobs so that they could wire cash back to their struggling families—he knew about that. And these were the things he was reminded of when his wife, a woman with a Jewish surname who had been born to street musicians in Portugal, cooked a pot of beans the way his father, a Muslim from Macedonia, used to do it. Beans were always a cheap source of protein. Meat was expensive. Meat was a luxury.

All of which is to say that the chief architect of the New Nordic movement had a complicated relationship with what would stereotypically be seen as Nordic. When he was profiled in *The New Yorker* by Jane Kramer, she brought this up with the chef. "When I told Redzepi about a blog I'd read, calling him a Nordic supremacist, he laughed and said, 'Look at my family. My father's a Muslim immigrant. My wife, Nadine, is Jewish. She was born in Portugal and has family in France and England. She studied languages. If the supremacists took over, we'd be out of here.' "

The Bronx

IMAGINE THE BRONX IN THE 1980S. IMAGINE THE sidewalks. Imagine the sneakers. Imagine the music. In the Bronx at the red dawn of the Reagan years you've got the genesis of a way of being—a way of expressing oneself—that will, within a few years, gather momentum and become ubiquitous around the world: hip-hop. Block parties in the South Bronx have led to new milestones in the ongoing story of black excellence. Microphones and turntables—songs derailed and deconstructed to allow for the free flow of message. DJs and MCs—everybody has something to say and mouths are open, ears are open, it's time to say it.

Malcolm Livingston II was born in the Bronx on August 13, 1986. It's all too easy for people who don't know the Bronx to dismiss Livingston's place of birth as a "war zone," as the usual media cliché would have it. Livingston will always know otherwise. To him and his friends, the Bronx hums with cultural vitality—the energy of family and community, brotherhood and beats.

That said, for a kid with a talent for identifying and transmuting flavor, it is an unusual place to grow up. Fine dining doesn't prevail here in the Pelham Parkway neighborhood, one of the various areas that formed him. Fast food dominates. Choices usually come down to which corporate franchise you want to patronize on any given day— Popeyes or KFC, Burger King or McDonald's or White Castle. Sure, Jamaican beef patties and Dominican plantains and Guyanese roti scent the doorways on certain blocks, but in comparison to the innovation and sheer plenitude of culinary options a subway ride away in Manhattan, the boogie-down borough is, well, kind of a wasteland. Sometimes you couldn't even find fresh fruit in the bodegas. Here you have Malcolm Livingston's dilemma— and, paradoxically, the source of his drive. He's not an MC, but he's gifted nonetheless. Livingston was born in the Bronx with a genius-level palate.

"It's really hard to describe how I come up with dishes," Livingston says. "I know what tastes good." He is getting ready to move to Copenhagen to become the new pastry chef at Noma, and he's prepared for whatever thought experiment Redzepi might throw his way. "If he said 'Make a dessert out of fish bones,' that might be a little hard. You're not going to make an ice cream out of it. If he says 'Do something with onion,' onions are so sweet. Apples and onion. Apples and shallots. Apples and shallots and beer. I could go on for days with just flavors. All of that came from working at wd-50. I've got to give credit to Wylie. I'll never think of food the same way after working with him." Wylie is Wylie Dufresne. Before getting the job offer from Noma, Livingston spent some time as the pastry chef at Dufresne's wd-50 on the Lower East Side of Manhattan, where cooking felt a lot like chemistry class at an especially psychedelic college. "You ever heard of volatile compounds?" Livingston says. At some point he got a book about volatile compounds from the New York University department of food science—a book that helps explain why, say, honeydew melon and jasmine and cucumber might play well together. "That's how I'm able to break down unusual flavor combinations," he says. "That's kind of how I break down food."

Another way to think about it: sampling. Dropping one track into the middle of another track, making sure they're in the same key, hearing them merge. Bringing the innovations of the Bronx to the arena of world cuisine. "I correlate hip-hop to cooking," Livingston says. "You gotta know how to mix, chop, and make a beat." He can freestyle and figure out what to pair with anything. Connections and cross-pollinations—he could do this in his head, in the air, without even a spoon or a stovetop. But he was doing that long before he owned a book about volatile compounds. It began—his awareness of it—years ago, when he was still a kid.

Imagine a kitchen in an apartment high enough to give him views of the surrounding blocks. That's where Livingston had the famous banana pudding—in the home of his octogenarian aunt, Alice Pulley, a churchgoing lady with roots in Virginia. She'd grown up on a farm with peanuts, tobacco, cotton, cucumbers, watermelon, apples, and peaches, and when she moved to New York in the 1950s, she brought that knowledge—that connection with fresh produce—to her cubicle of a kitchen.

"Anything you see in a garden, we had it," she'll tell you. Outside there may have been crack vials scattered around in the parking lot, remnants of the worst part of the crisis a few years earlier, but up here in Aunt Alice's apartment young Malcolm and his crew found an array of cakes and pies that would rival a pâtisserie in Paris. "They would come over. 'Auntie, where are the goodies?'" she recalls. "Whatever they asked for, I would try to fix it for 'em." For a kid with a future as an international pastry chef, studying at Alice's elbow was as good as a master class at the Cordon Bleu.

"I remember that pound cake—so moist, but so dense!" Livingston says. "Eating her food for the first time—it wasn't processed food. My palate was developing really early. You see, it all started here." The conversation with

Aunt Alice has never really stopped. They're still talking about flavor, still figuring out what tastes good together. Take sweet potato pie. It's perfect. But can it become something even better than perfect?

"I don't want to change the flavors of sweet potato pie, because there's nothing wrong with it," Livingston muses. That said, what if you were to pair it with tamarind?

"How about throw some corn flakes in there . . . ," Aunt Alice chimes in.

"That's a dessert right there," Livingston says. "Corn flakes, sweet potato, and tamarind." Autobiographical, too, simultaneously touching on the Caribbean, the American South, and a bodega in the Bronx.

Without his family's passion for food, Livingston might never have found his way into some of the top kitchens in New York. His mother came from Barbados and had that connection to "fresh fruits, island fruits." At home there was chicken with jerk spices and, during the holidays, the Caribbean thirst quencher called sorrel. (Anise, grapefruit, hibiscus, Campari—years later, Livingston would figure out how to tweak sorrel, and tap into those volatile compounds, in coming up with a dessert that he made at wd-50.) His mother would roast a chicken, give it a good sear, then pair it with coconut rice and peas. "She'll do this coleslaw—man, I'm telling you," he remembers. "Plantains—we always had plantains." Meanwhile his father was a raw vegan. This was a family who took food seriously, so how could Malcolm Livingston II do anything less?

There were blind spots, of course. "I didn't grow up eating foie gras and sturgeon caviar," he remembers. "We didn't go out to eat a lot, and if we did, we didn't get dessert. When I went to France I had a strawberry and I thought it was fake. I thought they had sprayed something on it." Imagine it's four in the morning and you've got to get to the kitchen at Per Se, Thomas Keller's stately sanctuary in the Time Warner Center on Columbus Circle in Manhattan. You've got to rush, you've got to switch from the Bx12 bus to the D train, and the D train takes forever. Imagine how it feels when your talent for flavor—your innate understanding of volatile compounds—helps to open the door to Le Cirque and Per Se and eventually wd-50. Well, at wd-50, Livingston had sort of slipped in the door on his own. On Sundays, his days off uptown, he would head downtown to hover and observe as wd-50's pastry visionaries (including Rosio Sánchez, his future predecessor at Noma) gave him lessons in the practice of mind expansion through sugar. He interned there and, as he puts it, "I stayed and kind of never left."

Do you want to move to Copenhagen and become the pastry chef at Noma? Imagine growing up in different neighborhoods of the Bronx and working your way to such an opportunity. The kitchen at Noma was full of stars that Redzepi had somehow identified around the world. Now it would be Livingston's time to imagine—to come up with flavor combinations involving ingredients that he has never heard of, let alone tasted. "Skyr—I've never had skyr," he says. "I'm really excited about the insects. All the different mushrooms. The herbs. The flowers. I've got to see what type of produce is out there. Maybe there is some banana flavoring in insects. Maybe there is some banana flavoring in herbs, in flowers. It just spurs so much creativity. You know what I would not want to make a dessert out of? Beef." But then he rethinks that. Maybe it would work after all. You can almost see the volatile compounds shifting positions in his mind. "I could do a bone marrow ice cream. Bone marrow cake. Bone marrow caramels. Bone marrow and tofu."

On his right hand Livingston has, in tattoo form, words from a famous utterance by another Malcolm: "By Any Means." (On his left hand: "Necessary.") On his ring finger the tattoo carries a chunk of his own surname: "Living." He's not going to lie—Copenhagen seems pretty far away, especially now that Livingston and his wife, Meeka Kameoka, are thinking about starting a family. "I've heard it gets really depressing—the fall weather. I've heard it gets really dark. I'm going to try to bring that New York style to Copenhagen—bring the Bronx to Copenhagen," he says. "My whole family is religious. But I do believe in a higher power. I'm not really religious, but I felt like God is sending me here for a reason. It was ordained. It was supposed to happen."

"Now where you going?" Aunt Alice asks him, as he continues gazing out the window of her apartment, studying the horizon.

"I'm going to Copenhagen, in Denmark," he tells her. "I'm going to this restaurant called Noma. Which is basically the best restaurant in the world."

"Wow," she says. "Don't worry, you're gonna do good."

Part Two

BURNING DOWN
THE HOUSE

Copenhagen

what
destruction am I
blessed by?

—A. R. AMMONS, "Moment"

WELCOME TO THE NEW NOMA," REDZEPI TELLS ME.
The place is a pit. We're on the edge of Christiania, the lawless, carless precinct of Copenhagen known for its cheap hash. Thanks to a government edict in 1973, Christiania exists as a social experiment wedged into the middle of the city, a haven for slackers and squatters—locals call them the slumstormerene. Technically speaking, Redzepi has taken me to a patch of land that does not belong to Christiania, but the border is mere yards away, and from the looks of the scene in the late summer of 2015, this is where the collective wastebasket of Christiania tends to tip over and spill out.

The ground is clotted with broken bottles and dank slabs of asphalt. There is a small lake, and beyond it, an outline of smokestacks that call to mind a Pink Floyd album cover or Pittsburgh in February. Dominating the plot of land is a long empty warehouse, the sort of habitation in which you might imagine characters from Cormac McCarthy's *The Road* roasting a suspicious dinner over a campfire amid the toxic vapor trails of a global apocalypse. Everything about the place says "last gasp" instead of "new dawn." Graffiti has been expectorated on every square inch of visible surface area. Local skate punks are taking their desultory turns with a plywood ramp in the middle of the bunker. We listen to the wheels of their skateboards clomping up and down on their wobbly boards until the kids are finally shooed away like feral dogs. "People smoke a lot of weed here," he says. "People have raves here, too."

So, wait, what's going on?

Redzepi has brought me here, to this lump of sketchy real estate, to tell me that he has a plan. It's the same plan that he alluded to when we were hanging out in Mexico. It's a big plan, in true Redzepi fashion, and you might say it's an insane plan. He wants to close Noma, at least the Noma many have come to know and love—to dismantle the most influential restaurant of his time—and move it here, to the visual equivalent of an abandoned waste facility in Chernobyl. "What you have to imagine is that this will be a farm in the city," he says. "This here. What you're standing in, right here, will be the future greenhouse. There will be one big herb garden going all the way down. We'll build a raft and we'll put a huge field on the raft. When this came up, it was, like, perfect. The perfect scenario." Maybe they'll have livestock. Maybe there will be chickens nibbling and clucking around the property.

By now it has sunk into my head that René Redzepi

is a man capable of bringing impossible schemes to fruition, but this seems nuts. Also, why? Why undo everything that has taken years to build, and why undertake it in the midst of a planned Noma pop-up about ten thousand miles away in Sydney, Australia? As he stands on the grim tar-paper roof of the bunker and surveys the scraggly landscape, I feel a mix of awe and pity. What we are looking at, he tells me, is a farm. I see a befouled parking lot next to the sort of swamp you see along the New Jersey Turnpike. Redzepi sees a farm. If Noma aspires to the heights of locavore gastronomy, it will have to begin controlling production—growing its own vegetables. He envisions the glass-strewn, tar-warted acreage being replaced, over time, by rich and loamy soil. He imagines pontoons—actual rafts, as he says—extending outward across the surface of the lake and acting as waterborne organic gardens. Redzepi is Moses and this blasted death strip before my eyes will, by his hand, blossom into a New Nordic land of milk and honey.

Or maybe he's the Klaus Kinski character in Werner Herzog's *Fitzcarraldo,* possessed by a mad dream of erecting an opera house in the humid, buggy tangle of a South American jungle. With Redzepi, you never can tell.

But the question that will gnaw at me for a while is, again: *Why does he have to do this?* Yes, we occupy a time in history in which themes of disruption and reinvention are revered. We live in a period that makes the pace of instant gratification look slow. You can make a splash, these days, and be forgotten six months later—the culture, horse-whipped by social media, loses interest if you don't keep blowing up the story. All of that said, couldn't the guy just coast for a while? Redzepi had raised Noma from obscurity through years of obsessive labor. Many times, while foraging, he had felt his throat going scratchy because he had plucked a toxic leaf that was not meant to be ingested. He had weathered nights when the dining room was nearly empty, had pushed his team through tortured passages of innovation, and had broken through to the moment where Noma was recognized as the peak of international cooking. One night he glimpsed at the waiting list and saw ten thousand names on it— ten thousand people on deck for dinner. Still, he had almost lost it all in 2013, when the norovirus outbreak among Noma's customers had threatened to detonate the status he had worked so hard to shore up. Why not just stand still for a year or two, breathing in the fresh air and savoring the landscape?

On the way over to the future location, Redzepi had provided some reasons. Everyone in Copenhagen rides a bicycle. Go for a stroll in the city and it is not uncommon to watch hundreds of two-wheelers as they spin through the city en masse—many of the riders so beautiful that, here, a Viggo Mortensen or an Alicia Vikander would probably just blend in with the crowd. Even babies are ferried around in this way, usually in square wooden boxes that are affixed to the front of the bikes like grocery baskets, and it is into one of these mobile tubs that Redzepi has placed me for my tour of the city. I scrunch my way into the box and he chauffeurs me around town as if I am a street urchin. Along the way he tells me about how everything is changing. A bridge is being built from

Nyhavn—the most tourist-Instagrammed strip of the harbor—to the quiet pocket of Christianshavn where Noma has bloomed in relative isolation for years. The foot traffic over that bridge will stir up the tranquil currents of the Noma oxbow. Meanwhile now when he walks into the Noma kitchen all he sees are limitations. The space was never meant to house an international beacon of cuisine, let alone the headquarters of a revolution, and the Noma team has outgrown it.

But the bridge is an ancillary concern. What is really going on with Redzepi has to do with the way he's wired. I can see it in his eyes. For some people, the need to keep moving and changing is so all-encompassing that it becomes an itch that can't be scratched away. Merely having a great restaurant isn't enough. He needs Noma to be even better than it has been—"Even though it's been successful, even though it's had media attention and all that, we're just finding our way," he tells me—but more than that, he needs to leave something behind. While Redzepi and I stand on the perimeter of the ragged lot, he picks up a pebble and uses it to scribble the number 12 in the dirt. Then he puts a zero in front of the 12. I can't figure out what this means at first. He's referring to the number of years Noma has been open, but he's employing it as a way of seeing. "It's hard to believe that twelve years ago"—when Noma opened—"there was no Twitter. No Facebook. No Instagram. Who knows what happens in twenty years? In thirty years?" He doesn't think of a twelve-year-old restaurant as an older establishment. He thinks of it as a young restaurant, its brain and limbs still developing. Pretend

you're looking at an odometer or a digital scale. You have
to add the zero in order to let yourself think in terms of
centuries instead of decades. "I feel that we are infants in
our life span," he says. "If you put a zero in front, you foster
that kind of long-term thinking. We should make deci-
sions that make this evolution last for 912 years."

We could theorize as to why the son of a Macedonian
Muslim immigrant—a man whose father senses the glare
of discrimination whenever he boards a city bus—would
want to leave a millennium-long imprint on a metropolis dominated by the blond descendants of Vikings. Right
along the side of the bunker that will house Noma 2.0 there
runs a dense mound of soil crowned with vegetation. This
is a remnant of an ancient fortress "set up to protect Denmark from invaders," Redzepi tells me, and the symbolism
is hard to resist. It may've taken centuries, but one of those
"invaders" has done an end run around the walls and the
moats, giving this Scandinavian stronghold a dose of the
innovation that only an outsider can deliver.

He knows he could coast. But he's allergic to coasting.
"I could take it easy at Noma," he says. "Do another menu
so there's a little more choice. That would relax a lot of people." Noma would eventually fade into the past, become a
legend in the world of food, like El Bulli or Lutèce. Or he
can aim for something more ineffable and impossible—a
restaurant that achieves a sort of cultural permanence.
"For that you need to be daring," he says. "All the time.
It really, really, really, really makes me nervous. I'm not
afraid. But it does make me nervous. I think the last six
months of the old Noma will be very popular reservations."

And after that? Everyone jumps off a cliff. First Noma will decamp to Sydney, Australia, for a pop-up using indigenous ingredients, then the old Noma will careen toward its finale, and then . . . *tabula rasa.* How often does anyone get to start over?

"We're not looking to change the very spirit of who we are," Redzepi says. "We're amplifying it. From day one we're not going to be perfect. It's probably not going to be as good as the old Noma was at the end. But give it time and we will be better. Much, much better. An even better restaurant. A more profound experience. An even deeper understanding of ingredients." Broken down into three distinct seasons (seafood in the winter and early spring, the plant kingdom in the summer, wild game in the fall), the Noma menu that Redzepi is dreaming about won't repeat a single dish or idea from the previous playbook. He's been thinking about time—he's inspired by the Long Now Foundation, the San Francisco–based institution devoted to shifting human thinking so that people consider, and plan for, the farther-out ripples produced by a pebble dropped into a pond. He wants more than what's merely immediate. "Of course we could just continue as is," he says. "Just stay put and do what we do there. But I genuinely think we won't progress." Maybe his children will inherit Noma. Maybe it will flourish under his great-grandchildren. Redzepi is playing a long game.

"It's going to be a complex of innovation and exploration," he tells me as he surveys his pockmarked little wasteland. And the way he says it, you believe him—hell, you want to grab a shovel and start digging. "It makes sense to do it here. It makes sense to have your own farm, as a restaurant of this caliber." On the surface it makes no sense, of course, but Redzepi doesn't see what you see. He looks at a field of flowers and weeds or a dune tufted up with beach grass and he sees the produce aisle at your local supermarket—an edible display. It's the same here. He envisions a world-class restaurant where you see a ruin. "As long as I can remember, it has been a derelict building," he says. "But imagine that this, here, is the kitchen." And *imagine this,* he says—stop talking, close your eyes, and imagine the wildlife that surrounds you, hiding in plain sight. "Just be quiet," he says. "You're in the fucking city, my friend." Ducks quack. Birds tweet. Insects hum. Leaves rustle. And he says, "It's like a little sacred haven."

Redzepi goes around back, by the ancient mound, and climbs up onto the tarpaper roof of the bunker. He walks up to the very edge of the roof. For a moment I worry that the greatest chef in the world is going to go tumbling over the side, onto the pavement. "That's how it feels," he says. "You're right on the edge, looking down. I have yet to meet anyone who thinks this is a stupid thing." In Zen Buddhism, teachers talk about the wisdom of seeing the world, when you can, from the perspective of a "beginner's mind." Even if you've seen it countless times before, you hit reset and see it anew. Up there on the roof, Redzepi is trying to see the future through just such a lens—at least until his impatience gets the better of him.

"Let's walk," he finally says to me. "I can't stand still like this."

Sydney

TO GET USED TO THIS LIFE YOU HAVE TO GET USED TO airports. Instagram overflows with images of the destinations that have been reached—the hotel beds as inviting as layer cakes, the mountain vistas, the cobblestoned alleyways—but to savor these delights you must pass through a series of terminals. How you feel about airports, and airplanes, might determine how suited you are to such an existence. Do you like to remove your shoes and your laptop after inching through the serpentine spirit-killer that is the security line? Do you like trying to figure out where to place your carry-on bag when you need to use the airport restroom but the floor is speckled with schmutz of dubious provenance and you can't find a hook because all the hooks seem to have been snapped off? Do you like to occupy a seat the size of a birdcage for, say, eleven hours at a stretch? These are minor inconveniences in the sweeping tragedy that is life on earth, I know. They accumulate in the mind, though, and they come to counteract the intoxicant rush of getting away.

And travel *is* an intoxicant, particularly for those of us who loathe the sedimentary layers of undone to-dos that pile up at home like domestic fossils. Insure the jewelry.

Call the plumber. Shred the documents. Send the check. Reschedule the orthodontist. Install the virus scanner. Investigate the possibility of identity theft. Call the cable company about the weird overcharges. Seek out marriage counseling. Find the right divorce mediator. Solve custody issues. Split up the 401(k). Join a gym. Or, better yet, don't. Postpone it—all of it. Get on a plane and wake up somewhere else. Italy. South Korea. Portugal. Patagonia. Newfoundland. New Orleans. An editor proposes an idea and you say yes without preemptively untangling the logistics—hell, the logistics will untangle themselves, just like the marriage and the money. The lure of travel will take you far away from the realm of clogged toilets and Con Ed bills. *That's awfully irresponsible,* you say? You're right. I daresay that's the point.

I always disliked the word "escapist," but maybe that's because it nestled a little too close to my skin. The truth is that for years I managed to turn escapism into a source of income. Real escapism must be left to the professionals, and I am honored to count myself among them. It's not impossible that I was drawn to journalism in the first place because I cottoned to the idea of having subsidized adventures. (The notion of doing something meaningful came later, which is undoubtedly an ass-backward approach, but I feel compelled to be candid here.)

For an escape junkie such as myself, meeting Redzepi was like introducing an alcoholic to the world's most telepathic bartender. How else to explain the thousands of dollars that would spiral down a drain as I started to say yes to one escapist punch bowl after another? Dinner in Sydney? Why not? Fishing in Norway in winter? Oh, absolutely. A graduate-level immersion course in the art of Mexican mole, just outside of Oaxaca? *Yes yes yes, where's the plane, get me out of here.* I could find and book a cheap flight in a matter of minutes.

But with Redzepi, the superficial thrills of a great escape would, over time, yield to deeper resonances. When I met him, he was on the cusp of blowing up his secure foundations in a campaign to reinvent himself and his restaurant. So was I—in, albeit, a far more haphazard fashion. But by the time I went to Australia, I had snapped out of the walking trance and my life had begun to take on some semblance of forward progress. This time, on the flight to Sydney, I had someone in the seat next to me who wasn't trying to knock my elbow off the armrest. I had known Lauren for years, on a professional basis, because I wrote about chefs and Lauren worked for a company that did publicity for chefs, and for this stark reason (not to mention the fact that we were for years both in relationships with other people) we maintained a safe professional distance. Steering clear of her, though, proved to be difficult, because we moved in the same circles in New York City and because I found her to be breathtakingly beautiful. (Distance itself would play a role in our eventual courtship. By the year of our flight together to Sydney, Lauren was living in Los Angeles. We corresponded like two global nomads from the 1920s, sending each other a constant flurry of postcards.)

Over the years I got to know Lauren, through conversation and emails, and I became captivated by her sophistication and composure. I had mentally filed away this crush as one of life's many impossibilities, but during this time in my life I was coming to learn that impossibilities weren't always as impossible as they seemed. One night in the summer of 2015 when I was watching TV with my daughter, a random texting exchange with Lauren took an unexpected turn. She was at Fish & Game, a restaurant up in Hudson, New York. I recommended the roast chicken. It was revealed that both of us happened to be single. It was suggested (I believe by her) that we should go out to dinner sometime. I agreed.

"Tomorrow?" Lauren said.

Bold immediacy—I liked this approach very much. We met the next night for a feast at Via Carota, in the West Village, after which we learned that our chemistry was more uproariously real than we'd imagined it. Somehow we soon became inseparable, even though I lived on the East Coast and she was moving (a week after our first date) to Los Angeles to open her company's West Coast bureau. Another perceived impossibility. We flew to Sydney from Los Angeles, in fact—when I told her that I had a table at Noma Australia, she wasted no time in suggesting that we spend a week in Sydney together—and I soon realized that the hopeless escapist in me had found a partner in crime. Lauren was all about saying yes to adventure, obstacles be damned. We landed in Sydney on Valentine's Day. The first text I saw, when I turned on my phone, was a "welcome to Australia" one from Redzepi. He wanted to know where we intended to eat. I told him I had no idea; I figured that it would be impossible to score a table anywhere decent on Valentine's Day, so we'd probably just get room service in the hotel. About five minutes later, an email appeared on my screen confirming that Lauren and I had a table at Bennelong, a restaurant tucked inside the famous Sydney Opera House, with a view of the harbor. Redzepi had contacted Bennelong on our behalf. But if I thought this trip was going to be all about luxurious moonlit dinners, I was mistaken.

The call came late in the afternoon.

You could hear a note of panic on the other end of the line. Someone from the kitchen in Sydney had run out of watercress. They needed the watercress as part of a wild green bouquet that accompanied a plate of abalone schnitzel. The first dinner seating would come together in a matter of hours, with guests who had flown in from all over the world to experience René Redzepi's sorcery with the ingredients of the Antipodes, and an arrow in the quiver could not be found.

"I'll be back around five or five thirty," E.J. Holland said. "Nobody all day has told me. The only thing anybody asked for was sticks. If they need something important, they need to say it."

"I can never get through to you," the voice from the kitchen barked.

"My phone's a piece of shit, bro," Holland replied. He agreed to turn around and hunt for some watercress. He hung up. He looked at the cars filling the roads as rush hour approached. "Traffic," he muttered. "This is not a good sign."

Time was running out. This wasn't just a matter of stuffing a box full of random wild clumps. The kitchen had high standards. Usually a more persnickety culling would take place in the kitchen, but tonight no one would have the bandwidth for that. "I'll just look very carefully at the quality when I'm picking it," Michael Larsen said.

Larsen and Holland were the leaders of Noma's foraging unit in Sydney and around the rest of Australia, and they made an unusual duo. Larsen, gentle and wry and connected to Noma from early on, came across as the walking embodiment of a Wendell Berry poem. He seemed so plugged into the rhythms of the plant realm that the close proximity to photosynthesis had given him a deep core of calm. Merely chatting with him felt nourishing. Holland, on the other hand, acted like the trigger-happy young turk in a Hollywood buddy comedy—the brash sidekick in foraging, hyper-voluble and slightly unhinged. He did not say "I will bring you your fucking watercress, but there'd better be a bottle of tequila waiting for me when I get there," but if he had, it would not have been out of character.

The Australia pop-up was the second of three residencies that would change the way Redzepi cooked—and thought about cooking. The first had happened in Japan and after it, he said, Noma would never be the same. "The impact from Japan? It keeps going. I think it influences us for sure. The *meaning* of everything in Japan. Everything has a purpose. Everything you eat has a reason for being

on the plate. It's as if everything they eat is at the right
moment. It gives such value to even the simplest of things.
Mostly I went to Japan to be inspired for innovation. How
does innovation move in such a place where tradition is so
deep? How come here in Denmark so many of the tradi-
tions have become old and stale?"

Australia was a different game entirely, though. In
Australia the Noma team wasn't coming up against centuries of culinary tradition as much as it was attempting
to wring deliciousness out of a slate of antipodean food-
stuffs that might as well have been tubers and seeds from
Venus and Mars. In Japan, Redzepi told writer Tienlon Ho,
"I wanted to show locals the foods they didn't even know
were part of their own place." In Australia, he was dou-
bling down on that gamble and venturing into the realm
of mangrove snails and konkleberries, yabbies and mulga.
"The test kitchen proceeded with more projects—a miso-
marinated banana, tongue-numbing mountain pepper
berries steeping in various vinegars, fermented eggplant,
ice creams of gum tree and myrtle, crispy crocodile skin,
and muttonbird wrapped in saltbush and grilled," Ho
wrote of the process of perfecting the meal that Noma
eventually wanted to serve. "Redzepi knows his ingredients can sound off-putting."

The trick was to transform that repulsion into attrac-
tion. The Noma Australia menu achieved this in part by
serving dishes that had a touch of lowbrow fun to them:
a slice of cake, a slab of schnitzel, a popsicle. The popsicle,
from Malcolm Livingston's pastry sector, was called the

Baytime, an allusion to a popular Aussie Good Humor–style street treat called the Golden Gaytime, only this one had peanut milk in place of vanilla-and-toffee ice cream, and a buttery glaze of toasted freekeh instead of a chocolate coating.

The schnitzel didn't broadcast this fact, but it was a fine example of Noma's latest journeys along the countless tributaries of fermentation. Coaxed into tenderness with a braise in rice koji oil, the schnitzel had a funky crust in which bread crumbs joined forces with rice koji flour. (Koji, hailing originally from Japan, "refers to rice or barley that has been inoculated with *Aspergillus oryzae,* a species of fungus—a sporulating mold, to be exact—that grows on cooked grains in warm and humid environments," according to *The Noma Guide to Fermentation.*) To me it resembled a Seder plate from one of Saturn's moons, the crispy-battered half-disk of abalone surrounded by a green orbit of native delights, a few of which were obscure enough that most Australians would never consider eating them. Lauren and I ate Neptune's necklace, a seaweed whose briny pods pop in your mouth, and finger lime, whose minuscule capsules offer a contrasting squirt of tart citrus. We ate mat-rush, which grows along the coast and looks like a leek, and a bunya nut, which may have once been a dinosaur snack, and a morsel from a tree called the Atherton oak.

The person responsible for tracking down a lot of those goodies was this man driving the car, Elijah "E.J." Holland. Of all the Noma cultists that I met in my trips around the world, Holland struck me as the wildest of the true believers. He burned with the zealotry of youth—he was still only twenty-three—and he carried himself with percolating, Red Bulled bravado. Months earlier, when Holland had heard from a friend that Redzepi was coming to Sydney and needed to recruit a local forager, Holland had introduced himself to the chef by bringing along two hundred and fifty samples of wild edibles from Sydney and the countryside. "I went kind of nuts," he told me. "I think my head nearly exploded." The next day, Redzepi had dropped into Holland's restaurant, the Powder Keg, and had noticed "heaps and heaps of wild lemon aspen, like a jackpot." Normally lemon aspen comes to a kitchen frozen, but Holland had managed to locate bushels of it growing wild.

Redzepi saw the tart, tiny fruits and said, "I want that." He asked Holland to preserve it all for a to-be-determined role on the Noma Australia menu.

What had impressed Holland more than anything was Redzepi's approachability. "He talks to me as if I'm a mate, which is really cool," Holland said. "I've had his books for ages." And now Holland had been sent forth to scour the land, to harvest deliciousness from the beach cliffs and suburban shrubs of Sydney. He did so while carrying a long, serrated blade and forsaking the constriction of a shirt, meaning that more than a few urban dwellers, during the weeks of Noma's residency in Australia, might have spied a barefoot, muscular, tattooed man hopping through their backyard bushes with a knife.

A call could come at any time. *Could you find us six of those wild figs that we tried the other day?* Holland could. I accompanied him as he bounded into a small public park fringed by the hum of a suburban neighborhood. There he pointed out sandpaper figs, which sprouted directly out of the trunk of a tree. He sliced them loose with his knife and dropped them into a bag. Those figs—utterly negligible to the people who lived yards away from them—would be incorporated into a dish at the best restaurant in the world. But figs and watercress constituted the more conventional side of Holland's foraging portfolio. Much of what he and Larsen went hunting for would be thoroughly alien to an American diner—or even to an Australian one. In his vehicle Holland had a copy of a book by Jennifer Isaacs titled *Bush Food: Aboriginal Food and Herbal Medicine*, a guide to indigenous ingredients that had sustained people for centuries but that, at this postcolonial stage in Australia's history, remained invisible to the untrained eye and the westernized palate, even with chefs like Kylie Kwong and Ben Shewry bringing more attention to them. Holland wanted to learn as much as he could about what the continent's original inhabitants had relied on to stay alive.

He noticed these nourishments everywhere. Driving along the highway, with Bob Dylan's "Tangled Up in Blue" playing on the car radio, he saw food tucked away and tufting out of curbs and on-ramps. "Every single person walks by them every day," he said. "Those are peppercorn trees—they're covered in pink peppercorns." Holland had been foraging for much of his life, eating wild fennel and fallen apples as a kid, prone to chewing on the stems of waterlilies during camp hikes in the Blue Mountains. His mother would make aloe vera poultices at home; theirs was a home in which feverfew was used to cure migraines and dandelion roots were brewed into a tea to relieve nausea. His engagement with the world could be viewed as a version of synesthesia: instead of seeing colors when he heard music, he tasted flavors when he saw colors. "There's loads of wild garlic flowers coming in," he said. "Wait till you see some of the spots we're going to today. Mushroom season has just started. Saffron milkcap mushrooms—they're absolutely gorgeous." He knew of places in the Blue Mountains where "there are so many mushrooms I have to be careful where I'm walking."

To ride shotgun with E.J. Holland was like hearing fragments of *Alice's Adventures in Wonderland* recited aloud by the leader of a boy band. "These are lillypilly," he'd say, revealing a palm full of sour red berries and nudging you to sample one. "This is rambling dock. This'll smack you in the face. . . . See this? All these leaves? That is beautiful wild ginger. . . . This is Neptune's necklace and that is Norfolk Island hibiscus. . . . Bladderwrack—this is really, really lovely pickled. . . . This is known as sea rocket or beach mustard. Imagine that on a steak or a nice fatty piece of fish. And it's on every Australian beach! . . . This is called slender celery. It's wild celery. I want you to have a taste."

He stopped the car along the side of the road to gather herbs and he drove to the shoreline to wade into the surf and gather seaweed. On a beach at low tide he carefully stepped farther out into the ocean to check the crab traps, brandishing a spear that he hoped to hurl at passing stingrays. He did not seem held back by the usual laws of gravity or the amygdala and its regulation of fear. If given the

directive to harvest bunya nuts, he would shimmy up the
trunk of a tree to get them. Foraging with Holland felt less
like a stroll through the fields than a televised scavenger
hunt.

In all of these ways Holland lived up to the ideals of the
Noma cult. The enterprise known as Noma Australia was
never meant to be easy. It wasn't easy to organize, it wasn't
easy to get into (thirty thousand names were huddled together on the waiting list), and it wasn't necessarily easy
to eat. Even for someone familiar with the Noma ethos,
some of the dishes on the menu were almost willfully
strange. A pie, of sorts, made of dried scallops with lantana
flowers scattered on top. Clams, served at room temperature instead of being chilled, underneath a crispy amber
scrim of dried crocodile fat. Porridge of wattleseed with
saltbush. The wattleseeds, out in the wild, could only be
pried open by a brushfire: heat and smoke unlocked them
so that the meat inside could be eaten. Having no brushfire

at their fingertips in downtown Sydney, the Noma team had turned to dropping the wattleseeds into boiling water that had been infused with smoke and letting them bob around for hours until they relented. It seemed like a lot of work for a porridge.

Perhaps the weirdest ingredient in the Noma Australia larder was a rare fruit that could only be secured through Holland's reconnaissance. Monstera deliciosa, it was called. Delicious monster. Make of that name what you will. It looked like a large scaly phallus (why beat around the flowering bush?) and, when plucked unripe, it contained enough poison to kill you. It grew beneath low-lying palm fronds around Sydney, although it had originated far away in Mexico, and to reach a point of being both succulent and survivable, it had to be aged, in a sense, like cheese. Holland and Larsen would stack the delicious monsters in a box and bring them back to the Noma kitchen at Barangaroo Wharf. There the shafts would be individually wrapped in loose pages of newspaper and left to ripen on a shelf. Along the way the scales on the fruit would protrude and then begin to fall off. Ripening required two to three weeks. "René told me it's the most exotic-tasting fruit he's ever had in his life," Holland said. "I don't think anyone has ever put it on a menu in Australia."

Saturday Night Projects back in Copenhagen should have served as a clue. Redzepi viewed creativity as the by-product of constant pushing and pressure. It wasn't enough to fly your entire team to Australia and raise the funds to subsidize their housing for weeks. It wasn't enough to transplant Noma's signature dishes to Sydney and give them

a few locavore tweaks. Radical wholesale reinvention—
nothing else would suffice. The objective was to start with
nothing, to explode all preconceptions, and to conjure a
multitude of courses from there. If Saturday Night Projects
resembled *Shark Tank* crossed with *Chopped,* this was an
altogether different kind of game show, one in which the
easy route automatically qualified as failure.

Success meant this: a meal that had never been eaten
on earth, one that tasted simultaneously contemporary
and ancient. "What we are doing is not new," Redzepi told
me. "We are dealing with things that are as old as time
itself." For forty thousand years the people who inhabited
this continent had found ways to cook with what the landscape provided to them. "They've had a way of cooking
and surviving for thousands of years." The task was vast
because the land was vast. "Here in Australia, there's so
much," he went on. "It's like sourcing from Denmark to
Morocco, Denmark to Jerusalem." Scour those acres, come
back to the kitchen, coax nature into singing a song no
one's ever heard—no big deal.

"To tell you the truth, it's the only restaurant in the
world right now where you can get this," Redzepi said.
"The element of surprise—how often do you actually get
to experience new things? That's fucking rare."

"They did sound a bit nervous," Holland said as he tucked
away his phone.

He knew where to find the watercress. But it was not
in the pocket of pastoral greenery I was expecting. Hol-

land's "secret" extravagance of watercress was spread out adjacent to one of the most famous and photographed sunbathing spots on earth: Bondi Beach. Watercress grew thickly on a rocky slope just around the bend from the primary spit of sand and surf. Holland and Larsen and their team spotted the clumps of flora and got to work. The cress sprouted out of wet crevasses in the rock—places where liquid sluiced through. Apparently that's why they call it watercress.

The foragers unholstered their pruning shears and scrambled up the hill. They snipped watercress at assembly-line speed, conscious in the back of their minds of the tempers likely to flare up in the kitchen if they pulled into Barangaroo Wharf too late. "To me, foraging is a skill set that's as important as learning to braise," Redzepi would tell me later. "It's so intricately a part of what we do. A mistake in the kitchen? You can't just call the grocer. You have to go *pick* the stuff."

Surf pounded and sprayed a few yards from the hillside. The sun started going down and the sunlight went fractal in the ambient sea mist. Joggers dashed by while the foragers kept bending and plucking.

When they sensed that they had enough, Larsen and Holland and their crew raced back to the car. They climbed in. Holland started the engine.

"Who. Is ready. For traffic?" he said.

"I can't wait," said Larsen.

Copenhagen

EVENTUALLY, IF YOU WORMED YOUR WAY DEEP enough into the Noma cult, you were invited to do the Workout. I say "invited" because participation in the Workout was theoretically a privilege. Let's say there was an advancement in the belief system of a religion that required you to pierce your own cheeks with a metal rod that was attached to a car battery. That, too, might be presented as a privilege.

So it was with the Workout. René and Nadine Redzepi had, in the name of longevity and vitality and a barely hidden masochism, availed themselves of a personal trainer named Johan Troels Andersen. As far as I could tell, Andersen seemed to emerge from no known school of exercise—not Pilates, not yoga. His approach to fitness might best be described as "primitive." Just as Noma itself had been founded on a philosophy of rustic, back-to-the-land resourcefulness, so the Workout hinged on making the best use of whatever was around. What was around in the Redzepi family's backyard in Copenhagen was, for the most part, grass and dirt, as well as tree branches and spare wooden beams from which a rope could dangle.

When I was invited to participate in the Workout, I said

yes primarily so that I wouldn't disappoint Lauren—or, for that matter, Redzepi. A Meryl Streep–level master of the imperceptible glance, he would from time to time shift his eyes in the direction of my gut, which looked like a centurion's breastplate that had slipped downward and melted—an occupational hazard for a food writer if ever there was one. Redzepi would say something like: *Now is the time, Chef, now is when you have to start exercising to keep yourself from falling apart later in life.*

Yeah yeah yeah, I'd mutter. I couldn't seem to make it a priority. Ever since childhood I have found it mortifying even to be in the presence of other people who are working out. Exercise may be noble, but it's embarrassing to watch people doing it. Their Lycra getups, their sweat towels, their cheerful spirits, their habit of reeling off numbers and, in yoga, woefully mispronounced Sanskrit words that are meant to convey something about personal superiority—I find the whole production ghastly, even though I realize that avoiding it will kill me. I did yoga for a while, then I let it peter out. I did meditation for a while, then I let that peter out. As I have written here, I do like to go on walks. Long walks. If it's walking you want, I can walk for hours on end.

But walking was not part of the Workout. As I found out when Lauren and I showed up at the Redzepi family courtyard one morning in the fall of 2016, the Workout emphasized more arduous forms of movement, such as scuttling back and forth on the grass like an upside-down crab or running back and forth on a dusty, pebble-strewn strip of ground. You had to run forward and you had to run backward, and you had to finish each sprint with a flash round of push-ups. Redzepi wanted the Workout to hurt. He wanted to feel the burn. He wanted results. He had experienced an epiphany about his health after throwing his back out while playing with one of his daughters, Genta. Plus he was perpetually exhausted. "I had always worked out when I was younger: I was athletic, I played soccer," he told the writer Lisa Abend in a *Men's Journal* article about the Workout. "But it had been about six years since I'd done anything, and I'd gained 20 to 25 pounds since my mid-twenties. I was up to 180. I wasn't fat, but I was soft. I looked at these other guys in the industry, people I knew who had heart attacks in their forties or had to go into observation for high blood pressure, and thought, 'That could be me. I'm almost 40. Now is when things go downhill.' "

Central to Andersen's New Nordic calisthenics was a militaristic series of dance moves known as the burpee—an innocent name for an agonizing punishment. The burpee worked as a sort of test: Even if you harbored memories of having been an athlete, and even if you felt certain that a remnant of robust health must be present somewhere in your body, the burpee would disabuse you of that notion. It looked easy. It was not easy. Its alternative moniker, the squat thrust, does a more efficient job of describing the countervailing forces of energy—the feeling that you were somehow pushing a wheelbarrow uphill while balancing a melon on your head and trying to use your feet to stop pebbles from rolling in the opposite direction. One burpee would make my eyesight go all splotchy. In the middle of one burpee, I'd feel as though I was going

to topple over from dizziness. That swirl of delirium that
sometimes overtakes you when you lean over to tie your
shoelaces? This was it times ten. At least it was for me.
The act of repeatedly dropping from a standing position
to the plank of a push-up, and then unwinding backward
and hopping upward with arms raised high? One burpee
and I thought I was having a stroke. I was nauseous and
loopy. I hated it.

So did Redzepi, apparently. Or he used to. "I hated
working out, every single moment," he'd told Abend. He'd
spent six months dreading it. The spirit of Saturday Night
Projects infected everything Redzepi did. Just when his
team seemed to have reached the brink of exhaustion, he
would jolt them with a fresh challenge: *make a new dish
right now in the middle of the night ... pack your bags, guys,
we're going to Australia ... say goodbye because we're blowing up the old Noma and leaving it behind.* His approach to
the Workout was no different. Just when I thought it was
over, I heard those fateful syllables—"Okay, buddy"—and
realized that the exhausting exertions of relay running
and rope-dangling had served as a mere prelude to the
main event, a simple game that I imagined dated back to
centuries uncharted. Surely the Vikings had sparred this
way in the sylvan glades in between bouts of burning and
pillaging. In this game, two players faced each other in
a crouch. At the appointed moment, the objective was to
scamper around until you felt like you were in a position
to slap the other person on the back of a knee. Harmless
enough—fun, even. Except that the price of losing was
steep. Each time you got slapped on the back of your knee,

you were required to pay with a burpee. Or maybe three burpees. Or ten. Those burpees could add up, especially if you, like me, were chosen to face Redzepi himself in the Viking grab-a-knee game. It would be an understatement to describe the man as a competitor. He roared into matchups like this with the rowdy vigor of a young Teddy Roosevelt. When it was over, my abs felt like they had been used as a bobsled.

> *When I came home to West Egg that night I was afraid for a moment that my house was on fire. Two o'clock and the whole corner of the peninsula was blazing with light, which fell unreal on the shrubbery and made thin elongating glints upon the roadside wires. Turning a corner, I saw that it was Gatsby's house, lit from tower to cellar.*
>
> —F. Scott Fitzgerald, *The Great Gatsby*

"Welcome to heaven," Redzepi says.

Evening is falling in slow motion over Copenhagen and Redzepi's backyard is aswarm with people. It looks like Georges Seurat's *A Sunday Afternoon on the Island of La Grande Jatte* crossed with the bacchanalian inside sleeve of the Rolling Stones' *Beggars Banquet,* the one in which Mick and Keith and company lounge like Renaissance noblemen around a table piled with meat and fruit. No wonder Redzepi's workout is so important to him. Without exercise, chefs are basically counting the days until the onset of diabetes and gout. We sit at long tables where bottles of wine and platters of food jostle for space. Some of us sit on the lawn. Redzepi is addressing the crowd. "Just be here," he tells the assembled group. "Just be. The best restaurant in the world is actually here. Tonight."

It's hard to argue with him on that point. Gathered in his yard—summoned together like the Avengers of cuisine—are famous chefs from around the world. Alex Atala from Brazil and José Andrés from Washington, D.C. (by way of Spain), Kylie Kwong from Australia and Jessica Koslow from Los Angeles, Jacques Pépin and David Chang, Danny Bowien and Bo Bech, Michel Troisgros and Daniel Patterson. It is a testament to his status that Redzepi has been able to persuade these people to travel to Denmark from as far away as São Paulo and Sydney for what amounts to a picnic.

Tomorrow brings the kickoff of the MAD Symposium, an annual convergence of chefs and food media illuminati who are intent on chewing on and hashing out the most pressing issues of the moment, but for sheer exuberance nothing under the MAD tents is likely to top the Valhalla-ishness of this under-the-radar A-list cookout. (Before it begins, Redzepi asks everyone to refrain from posting about it on social media. Miraculously, we obey.) Redzepi being Redzepi, it has been deemed insufficient for these chefs merely to meet up and eat. It's not even enough for them to cook. What transpires instead is a *Battle of the Network Stars*–style showdown with the chefs divided into pairs in the afternoon and instructed to deliver a delicious dish for the picnic by sundown. *Go.*

"Everybody cooks," Redzepi says in the courtyard before it gets rolling. "That includes you." He means me. I can't imagine what soupçon of expertise, or even basic competence, I bring to the party here, but I work up my courage (I don't want to be forced to do any more burpees) and volunteer as a deckhand for the coolest duo in the arena: Jessica Koslow, the Southern California pioneer whose restaurant, Sqirl, serves the most distinctive breakfast in America, and Kylie Kwong, whose flagship in Sydney, Billy Kwong, has won global praise for incorporating indigenous Australian ingredients into the Cantonese recipes of her heritage. That aha moment—the realization that you should use what grows around you—can be traced, for Kwong, to a single, specific moment. In 2010, Redzepi traveled to Sydney and gave a speech. Kwong was there, and she left with the flush of energy that accompanies any creative person's visualization of a breakthrough. "That's when I started using them," Kwong tells me, while holding a bowl and whisking a mix of white miso and cherry blossom vinegar. "The next day. The next day! René prompted me to create this revolution at Billy Kwong. It was a lightbulb moment for me—'who *is* this guy?' "

Here in Copenhagen, Kwong tells me that she is third-generation Australian but twenty-ninth generation Kwong; she can map her lineage back to the Song Dynasty. The moment of clarity at Billy Kwong came down to an embrace of these interwoven threads of identity. "René has really inspired me to open up so much, discover my Australian-ness and my Chinese-ness through food," she says. That means stuffing dumplings with warrigal greens and fashioning savory cakes out of saltbush instead of turnips; it means dishes like red-braised, caramelized wallaby tail. She uses these ingredients because they're local and they taste good—because the John Nash–ish insight into René Redzepi could be described as a kind of Magnum Terroir, the concept that the foods that grow near you are the foods that are the most desirable for this place and time. "To quote René, it's actually delicious," Kwong goes on. "From a gastronomic perspective, it actually works."

Kwong may be a visionary chef, but I am not. Before long it becomes clear that my primary role in this make-shift al fresco kitchen is to commit mistakes that amuse everyone else. Brisk, clear, and patient—up to a point—Jessica Koslow comes across as the consummate professional in the kitchen, at least based on my couple of hours of nodding and chopping at her side. She decides on her

dish—a salad—and gathers her ingredients from a game-
show display a few yards away and tells me what to do.
Which should be simple enough: grab these clumps of
mint and thyme and strip the leaves from the stems. I
do this dutifully, if clumsily, for a while, until a question
percolates in my mind. Koslow is standing to my right. I
should point out here that I tend to have an unruly habit
of gesticulating. My arms, at times, weave and bob like
snakes. "Chef?" I ask, and I turn to ask Koslow the question, and some bizarre quantum alignment of space and
time brings us to a rare and sudden intimacy: because of
my flailing forearms, my herb-scented right index finger
has gone sailing right up into her left nostril. I will forever admire Jessica Koslow for the kind look of forgiveness
in her eyes as I extracted my gesticulating digit from her
nose. She must be a nice person to work for.

Bo Bech, a lumberjack-proportioned flavor virtuoso
here in Copenhagen, indulges my blundering with similar
élan. (Being a food writer for *The New York Times* and *Es-
quire* means that when it comes to the possibility of being
on the receiving end of a fiery kitchen tantrum, I am my
own human shield.) Bech has teamed up with Atala, which
means that the most overtly macho duo in the bunch—
Bech with his supersized Viking scaffolding, Atala with
his tattooed forearms and feral Amazonian gaze—are
working alongside two women, Kwong and Koslow, who
keep their mise-en-place theatrics to a minimum. Maybe
it says something about the implied droit du seigneur of
male chefs that after an hour or so, Bech makes it clear
to me that I am now staging with him and Atala. "Jeff, I

need you," he says. I can't tell whether some kind of negotiation has gone down. Maybe I'm being stolen. Or maybe
Koslow, in the wake of my nose-probing mishap, has qui-
etly traded me to the rough boys. (*Take this amateur off my
hands,* I imagine her whispering. *He's slowing us down.*)
Either way, Bech will soon sour on my apprenticeship. As
I click into my servitude with the Bech-Atala crew, I see
before me a plastic tub full of celery greens. Bech is pouring a glass of water on the pale green leaves to wash them.
Easy enough, I think—I grab a glass and do the same. The
look in Bo Bech's eyes as I pour his portion of nicely chilled
white wine all over the celery greens is something I shall
not forget. Bech is, as I have indicated, a large man, yes,
but in this instant he appears mountainous, King Kong–
like, capable of swatting me across the face with a paw that
would most likely contribute to early-onset dementia.

Bech does not hit me, of course. "No, no, no," he says as
if scolding a toddler. He tells me to start over. He points
toward a sink, and to that sink I haul the tub of celery
greens and wash the wine off them. Bech rewards me,
when I return, as if he's tossing a treat to an obedient dog.
He is known in Denmark for creating complex bites com-
posed of no more than three or five ingredients. He creates
one of these on the spot. He takes a knife and cuts a slice
the size of an anchovy from the uncooked carcass of a lamb
that is being dressed for its date with a roaring fire. Bech
curls the sliver of raw lamb on top of a green, unripe strawberry and pixie-dusts the bite with sea salt. Then he places
the bite directly onto my tongue.

"Jeff," he says. "Raw lamb. That's Denmark."

There is a thing you learn about chefs when you spend time with them: Even though they may cook complex food, they revere simple food. The word "simple" is an incantation, music to their ears, and they long for anything that doesn't seem fussed over or full of itself. For Redzepi that simplicity was expressed through a pot of beans or a plate of tacos. After enduring a tasting menu in Copenhagen, David Chang would predictably head straight for a late-night dive called Kebabistan for a gooey, salty heap of shawarma. Francis Mallmann, on his island in Patagonia, relished a simple repast of Persian rice saturated with butter and crusty from a cast-iron skillet. Massimo Bottura might be spotted walking a block away from his Osteria Francescana in Modena, Italy, so that he could refuel with prosciutto, Parmigiano-Reggiano, bread, and wine.

The same principle is at work here in the Redzepi courtyard, with twin sets of toques marinating and chopping and spatchcocking dishes at whim. Nobody pays much attention to what has been cooked, and most of the dishes (a roast lamb, assorted salads) wind up reflecting that longing for simplicity. It's like a jam session at which famous musicians cover a bunch of folk songs. It's not really a competition. There is no prize at the end. Redzepi hands out no trophies. The dish that "wins," by informal acclamation, is the simplest one: a turbot, properly seasoned and grilled whole, cooked without fanfare by Olivier Roellinger, a French chef and gentle leftist known for having forfeited his three Michelin stars, in tandem with his son, Hugo. Redzepi grabs my arm and nods toward the fish. "That's what you don't want to miss," he says. He's right—the flesh

of the turbot is firm and light and steamy from the fire—
and as night falls I can't help but wonder whether someday
René Redzepi will be like Olivier Roellinger, a man who
has bypassed fame and found contentment on the side-
lines. No one can be hungry forever, after all.

Norway

I'M ON A BOAT ON THE WATER SOMEWHERE ABOVE the arctic circle in Norway.

I can't tell you precisely where, because Roderick Sloan wouldn't want me to, but even if I unwisely and uncharitably decided to blow his cover and reveal the GPS coordinates of one of his prime fishing spots, I would be unable to pin it down. The air out here, in the middle of February, is so cold that my iPhone keeps shutting down unless I tuck it into a pocket close to my chest. My fingers keep shutting down, too, so I can only jot notes by hand in fast, gloveless bursts, and even then the ink in my pen appears to have stopped flowing.

"This is my yoga," Sloan is telling us. "This is where I find my soul." He's standing in a second boat, swaddled in a puffy jumpsuit that protects his body from subzero temperatures. Flurries of snow shimmy around him. The small islands and peninsulas that surround our boats are caked with layers of snow and ice. The water looks dark blue and dark green, depending on the light, which is wan and short-lived at this time of year. I find myself thinking about how long I would survive if I were to topple over into the Norwegian chop. But Sloan does it on a regular basis.

He found a way to earn a living, and has shored up a modi-
cum of international fame, by diving into these chilly currents to haul up what he considers the freshest, purest
seafood available in Europe. "The next time you look at
seafood, the best stuff comes from here," he tells us, a
group of trembling chefs and journalists, in his barking
Scots burr. "Everything here goes into my mouth first.
Every box must be perfect. Every box."

I have come to Norway in the middle of winter because
of the dish that dazzled me the first time I ate at Noma: the
sea urchin with hazelnuts. That dish can be traced all the

way here to the isolated frosts where Sloan lives with his
Norwegian wife and their three sons. The Noma cult may
have no more passionate an acolyte than Sloan. The writer
Franz Lidz once described him and his profession this way:

> *What makes Sloan perfectly risible in the eyes of many
> is the precarious career he has carved. In weather that
> would be considered mild only on Neptune, he dives into
> the icy fjord to gather sea urchins, those wee beasties that
> look like squash balls encased in pine thistles. Sloan's
> aquatic treasure hunts for krakebolle ("crow's balls" in
> Norwegian) are as dangerous as they are daring. Waves
> are often treacherous; squalls, gusty; and storms can ap-
> pear in an instant.*

The first time I met him, at the MAD Symposium in
Copenhagen, Sloan was sitting on a bale of hay. I suspected
that he had had a few drinks, but with Roddie Sloan there
was no way of knowing—his contact with people seemed
heightened by a form of inebriation all the time even if
alcohol didn't happen to be involved. He proceeded to chat
with me, and taunt me, in a manner that made camara-
derie and hostility seem virtually indistinguishable. You
couldn't tell whether he wanted to hug you or smack you.
With his beard and his cockeyed glance and his Scottish
accent, he came across like Begbie in *Trainspotting* if Begbie had been played by Robin Williams in *Popeye* mode.
He was lovable and irascible, openhearted and easily of-
fended (or was that just an act?), sometimes all within the
course of a single sentence. As was the habit with members

of the Noma diaspora, he looked me in the eye and made an insane suggestion: *Come up to Norway in the middle of February and we'll go fishing.* By now I knew I would have to offer an insane reply: *Sure.*

Redzepi had made the same trip, of course. Sloan's respect for the chef was fortified when Sloan took him out in the boat one day for about six hours. The temperature had sunk to around 5 degrees Fahrenheit, but Redzepi was wearing sneakers instead of the thick boots Sloan always hounds his guests into wearing. In spite of this the chef didn't complain about the cold. "The loyalty between me and René is huge," Sloan had told me. "He never lies. He pays on time. He never does anything bad."

At first, the bond between Sloan and Redzepi had been forged over a shared love for a single ingredient: sea urchins. Sloan's urchins were so fresh—shipped out the same day they were caught, placed on a boat, then on a plane, and delivered alive to Noma's tanks by four in the afternoon—that they required no adornment beyond the milk and meat of raw, unripe hazelnuts. Sloan's discovery of a bumper crop of krakebolle happened to dovetail with the moment in global gastronomy when chefs suddenly couldn't get enough of them. As Lidz wrote in 2014,

> *In the brave new world of fine dining, the roe of the humble urchin—a shellfish once cursed as a pest to lobstermen, mocked as "whore's eggs" and routinely smashed with hammers or tossed overboard as unsalable "bycatch"—is a prized and slurpily lascivious delicacy. Unlike caviar, which is the eggs of fish, the roe of the ur-*

chin is its wobbly gonads. Every year more than 100,000 tons of them slide down discerning throats, mainly in France and Japan, where the chunks of salty, grainy custard are known as uni and believed to be an uplifting tonic, if not an aphrodisiac. The Japanese exchange urchins as gifts during New Year celebrations.

But Sloan's rise to fame as Noma's urchin wizard also coincided with a cruel stroke of fate. One day, without warning, his undersea stockpiles of urchins simply vanished. The oceans can be fickle, especially with the vicissitudes of climate change wreaking havoc on natural habitats. "Both fragile and destructive, the urchin is a tempest in an environmental seapot," Lidz has written. "In every corner of the planet, there seem to be either too few or too many. The French and Irish exhausted their resident stocks years ago. In Maine, Nova Scotia and Japan, urchin populations have been drastically reduced by overfishing and disease." All Sloan knows is that he went out in the boat one day, squeezed himself into his sixty-five pounds of scuba gear, plunged into the water, risking getting trapped in tangles of seaweed, and came back to the boat empty-handed.

The experience left him shaken. He still has a hard time talking about it, in spite of his usual bluster. "They're gone, man," he tells me in a near-whisper. "It's feast or famine." He has maps. The maps are supposed to lead him to clusters of thousands. There were magazine profiles about him. "All of a sudden every chef in the world wants my product," he says. "I go back to the ocean and the ocean is empty. How embarrassing is that?"

He had to break the news to Redzepi, had to tell his best customer that one of his most prized ingredients would no longer be available.

"That's a shame, Roddie," Redzepi told him. "What else have you got? I'll buy it all."

I was, by now, riding high on escapist delirium. Noma juice was like a case of Lapierre Morgon I couldn't stop pouring for myself, and it made for a potent buzz when coupled with the elixir of my having fallen in love with Lauren, the escapist Bonnie to my Clyde. After hanging out with Sloan in Norway, I located, online, a $33 flight from Oslo to Paris, and I booked it without a second's thought. The walking trance had turned into a manic dance. I flew to Paris to explore the natural wine bars of the 10th and 11th arrondissements—places like Le Verre Volé, La Buvette, Aux Deux Amis, and Septime La Cave that represented a casually revolutionary leap forward in our consumption of wine. The natural wine movement in France had found an ally in Noma, whose ethos of organic wildness lined up with the ideology of *le vin vivant.* Living wine, raw wine, natural wine—whatever you wanted to call it, it was meant to be made with minimal interference from human beings, and (if possible) none of the additives that were frequently used to manipulate the color, stability, and hue. What morphed the fruit was the yeast that flourished by itself in the presence of sugars—on the grapes, on the leaves, on the stems, on the walls of the cellar. This was terroir to the nth power: The land created the wine that told a story about the land. If you imagine an ancient Roman sybarite mashing up fruit and letting it ferment in an amphora, you're not far off from the beau ideal. To make wine this way was to run the risk of letting the wine go in a bunch of different directions based on a range of unpredictable elements, and it's not hard to

see how such a credo appealed to Redzepi. Noma's decision to serve natural wines had been a radical one at first,
but it had cleared a path for other restaurants and bars
around the world to start doing the same, from Frenchette
in New York City to Ordinaire in Oakland, California. All
that said, some kind of wild yeast was apparently at work
on the vineyard of my brain, too. I had by now quit my job
at the *Times* and sold my house in Westchester County,
and I suppose I had booked the flight to Paris because of
some remembered youthful exhilaration that I hoped to
reconnect with. I found it, too, as I stood on the expanse
of the Pont Neuf and surveyed the city at night and began
sobbing hard enough that it felt like another burpee. Few
things are as exhilarating as a wholesale unloading. I
knew the rush wouldn't last, but I was determined to rel-
ish it while I could.

**Ferran Adrià told this paper that after years at El
Bulli, it became extremely difficult to develop new
ideas. How about for you? Where do you go from here?**

*I think it is quite natural at a certain point you have
nothing more to offer. You will start repeating yourself
and in the worst case become some type of cliché. I can't
think of a restaurant where I haven't seen it happen.*

*I'm sure I can find inspiration again at some point,
and I can reboot myself creatively, in a new project and a
new frame of work, and somebody else can take over at
Noma. That is for sure my plan.*

Once you reach No. 1, of course, it's the beginning of the end.

—RENÉ REDZEPI INTERVIEW WITH

KATY MCLAUGHLIN, *Wall Street Journal*, June 2010

And then it's happening, Noma is ending, there's no turning back.

I arrive in Copenhagen from Paris just as the team at Noma is riding headlong into the final lunch at the original location on that Christianshavn dock, the cobbled-together, never-quite-big-enough place where manifestations of Redzepi's ambition orbited the building like space junk. The barbecue grills out back that could've doubled for a carnitas operation down an alleyway in Tijuana; the fermentation laboratory a few steps farther back that looked like a loading dock full of shipping containers in San Pedro. The "greatest restaurant in the world"—did people realize what a tottering, improvised pile the place was? Did people understand that many of those opulent nibbles emerged from a warren of rooms and nooks and tubs as ramshackle as a punk band's rehearsal space? Did people comprehend what a weird miracle the whole thing was? To emerge from out of nowhere—like Bob Dylan out of Hibbing, Minnesota—and change the cultural conversation for a while?

"If you want to keep your mind young, you have to keep moving," Redzepi tells me as I drop my bags and head into the kitchen. Just last Saturday he sank into a depression, a dark one, but today he's aloft; he says the trillions of

cells in his body are telling him it's the right move at the
right time. I'm expecting some sort of nature metaphor—
something about the seasons, the circle of life, renewal and
decay—but instead he tells me that the whole thing could
be compared to a jumbo jet. Imagine that Boeing 747's first
flight on February 9, 1969. Imagine the force and faith required to get the tonnage of one of those behemoths to
take wing. All of that weight, rising into the air. "We are
the jumbo jet," Redzepi says.

I am spun around in the kitchen and there are two
desserts that Malcolm Livingston has left on the counter:
a bowl of milk ice cream with a gamey paste of ants on
the bottom and a sweet-sour syrup of apple vinegar and
quince on top. Then, as a final flourish, a second treat: a
featherweight Danish pastry that's twisted and elongated
like a stretched-out curly French fry. Redzepi encourages
me to eat them. These are the last dishes that will go out
to the dining room in the old Noma. Everything that has
been built since 2003 will now dissolve like flakes of pastry
on the tongue. Maybe that fleeting quality is part of what
makes eating so euphoric. Take all the pictures you want.
Preserve them on Instagram. But no image can reconnect
anyone with the flavor of a dish, its contrasts of texture
and temperature, the way it collapsed beneath your teeth.
Thousands of meals contributed to Noma's rise to promi-
nence over the years—plate by plate, bite by bite, mur-
mur by moan—but everyone in the kitchen knows they're
about to become nothing more than a rumor: "Hey, did
you ever try the sea urchin with hazelnuts?"

There is a touch of chaos in the air. You can talk about

change in the abstract, but everything feels charged with extra layers of drama when the change finally arrives. Mads Refslund has flown to Copenhagen from New York, and Anders Selmer is here from across town to raise a toast to what Noma once was. Both were part of the crew that opened Noma in 2003. The three of them, Redzepi and Refslund and Selmer, pose for portraits together. As if the intensity of the crescendo were not enough, Nadine Levy Redzepi has just endured dental surgery and is speaking as if her mouth were stuffed with cotton balls. "Half of her face is completely numb," Redzepi says. "I'm, like, 'Nadine, why'd you have a root canal today? On a fucking Saturday? And *this* Saturday?!'"

There has to be a speech. Redzepi doesn't want to give one. He stands in front of the team, an hour or so before the dinner rush begins, and freezes up. He can't locate the words. Emotion overwhelms him. Thomas Frebel steps in.

"Well, then, maybe it's me, guys," Frebel says.

"Thank you," Redzepi says, the rasp of hoarseness in his voice.

"Everybody knows I don't like to talk too much— speeches and stuff like that," Frebel says. "But I think I'm talking for everyone in this room and everyone who has been part of this restaurant just to say thank you, René, for having us." The room erupts in wave after wave of woofing and clapping.

Again Redzepi tries to talk. "I promised myself that I would not do a long trip through memory lane because we will have the time to do that over the next two days, while we're partying . . . also because it would be too much . . ."

He stops midsentence with his hand on his hips. He shakes his head. Refslund steps up from behind him and grabs Redzepi around the neck and shoulders. The chef is crying. He tries again to say a few words.

"It would be too much because everything I have in life has come through here," Redzepi says. "My wife. My kids. My friends." His voice cracks. He pulls his apron up to his eyes to sop up the tears. "The reason why I told myself not to do this is because, you know, I want to kill it so bad at the next place. You know what I mean? It's a *very difficult step*—to break with something. But this is what I need to do, and this is where we think that we'll be able to do even more amazing things. I don't at all doubt that. I don't at all doubt that. Thank you. For the past thirteen years, it's crazy, I didn't expect it to be like this. There's two people here—they were part of the first service. And some of you've been part almost since day one. It's crazy."

He remembers people walking through the front door for the first time. He remembers shouting at people. All at once, he remembers breakthroughs and breakdowns.

"This place has given me insane amounts—insane amounts—it's unbelievable. I truly truly truly believe that what has made us is the sum of all of us. I know I'm on the magazine covers and all that. But I know you feel it from the guests, right? They all say, 'There's something more than the food. The food is great, but there's something more.' How many of you have heard this? Everyone! There's something more. And that something is what people do. It's something with people. And that to me has been the most amazing thing at Noma. It's all the people. So thank you for being here and listening to all my crap and my shit and my temper swings, my mood swings, you know? I know that I've been a dick. A lot. Thank you for bearing through it."

Suddenly the tone of his emotions shifts—from nostalgia to fervor.

"And Noma 2.0? I haven't had this feeling since I was with Mads like thirteen years ago. I almost can't control myself when I think of it. You've all watched me these days. I don't know where to stand. I feel like my head is about to explode. I feel like shaking people. I feel like cracking the wall. I feel like fucking going crazy. That's how much I want it. You understand? Have you ever felt that way, where you just fucking want to grab it?"

He scans the crowd and looks into the faces of everyone he works with.

"Okay. Now? Let's have a great service."

At the end of dinner, as the desserts are fussed over and sent out to the last table, the cooks in the kitchen pop the corks on some shaken-up bottles of champagne and spray Redzepi with the culinary version of a coach's Gatorade shower at the Super Bowl.

The next morning, Redzepi and Lau Richter and Ali Sonko and other folks from the restaurant gather around the iconic NOMA sign that's attached to the outside wall. They take it down letter by letter, a cheer rising from the scrum with each alphabetical amputation. The progression seems rife with meaning. NOMA becomes NOM, and then

NO, and then N, and then there's an emptiness, nothing more than holes in a wall. Some tourists wander by, probably having walked over the new bridge, to see what the fuss is all about.

"The restaurant is closed, guys," Redzepi tells the tourists. "We're about to rip it all down. It's over."

Part Three

HOUSES IN MOTION

Oaxaca

The foods of regional Mexico are in a gastronomic world
of their own, a fascinating and many-faceted world, but
alas, far too many people outside Mexico still think of
them as an overly large platter of mixed messes, smothered
with a shrill tomato sauce, sour cream, and grated yellow
cheese preceded by a dish of mouth-searing sauce and
greasy, deep-fried chips.

—DIANA KENNEDY, The Art of Mexican Cooking

Everybody started painting one hand Day-Glo and
opening it and sticking one vast vibrating Day-Glo palm
out at the straight world floating by comatose . . .
    Kesey held another briefing, and without anybody
having to say anything, they all began to feel that the trip
was becoming a . . . mission, of some sort.

—TOM WOLFE, The Electric Kool-Aid Acid Test

THERE WAS SO MUCH IN MEXICO. SO MUCH TO EAT, SO
much to learn about. So many ingredients—chiles,
spices, leaves, coconuts, insects, fruits—and so many

preparations. But if there were two elements of Mexican cooking that Redzepi felt he needed to tackle before he could embark on the pop-up in Tulum with any real confidence, they were tortillas and mole. One was seemingly the height of simplicity—corn flour and water mixed into the magic putty called masa and griddled into patties on a comal—and the other was the very prototype of complexity. To try to define mole was to lose one's grip on its definition. Mole was everything and anything. It was an infinitude of blended juxtapositions. You could say that mole was a sauce and you could say that it tended to incorporate chiles and aromatics. (But not always.) You could say that a mole distinguished itself from a salsa by virtue of its density, its meconium-like viscosity, its compression of multiple ingredients cooked slow and low, and you'd be mostly right, but not always. The very word "mole" felt like a code-switching trick of language used by the indigenous people as a method of perpetually throwing Spanish invaders off their tracks. Mole could be red. Mole could be yellow. Mole could be green. Mole could be black. Mole could be so black, in fact—conjured from the charred parchment of chiles that had been burned to the brink of outright ash—that it tasted like a Goth bisque. Imagine ingesting flakes of night.

Tortillas were tortillas. Mole was all negotiation, but tortillas were nonnegotiable. They came in different sizes and hues and gradations of thickness, of course, but their function remained central to the very existence of a Mexican meal. Perhaps it is a paradox all too applicable to a man as complex as Redzepi, but I never saw him master a tortilla. He tried and tried, watching as women in Mexico would deftly place coasters of masa on the comal, looking for hints as the masa would eventually bubble up as though it were being inflated by invisible elfin sorcerers. He didn't have much luck with them. His tortillas rarely if ever bubbled up. People called him the best chef in the world and yet you could see in his eyes the blunt, wistful realization that he'd never *get* the art of the tortilla the way a sizable portion of the female population of Mexico had mastered it.

Mole, though. Maybe he could do something with mole. Not something better per se. There was nothing better than a true Oaxacan mole—he knew that. But he could do a Noma version of a mole, maybe, as a gesture of love for the country he had to keep coming back to. A thesis behind Noma Mexico was that the perfection of traditional dishes like cochinita pibil and mole poblano could never be topped. There was no point in trying. (To attempt to "top" them would, of course, be colonialist and autocratic, and offensive in that regard, but it would also be . . . patently impossible.) The Noma way—in Japan, in Australia, and here in Mexico—was to strip vehicles back down to their component parts and try to rebuild them or reimagine them from the ground up. (At its best, the act of doing this would foster a sort of cultural conversation between different regions of the world.) First, though, you had to understand what you were taking apart. Taking apart mole was like taking apart a river. Mole was fluid and endless. Its very nature was elusive. You couldn't "get to the bottom" of it. It was more of a mosaic of sauces than a sauce per se, more a manifesto than an ironclad recipe, and yet mole meant to Mexico what pesto meant to parts of Italy and tahini meant to the Middle East. A great mole might have twenty, thirty, forty, or fifty ingredients, the potential proportions of each ingredient pretty much infinite, all of them like pieces of an edible jigsaw puzzle that, when completed, revealed a different image each time. Redzepi, a competitor at heart, remained haunted by the mole madre that chef Enrique Olvera had made him swoon over at Pujol—a kind of Earth Mother mole, aged and alive and almost incalculable in its sedimentary layers of spice and funk.

The quest would require more than one person. To spelunk in the ancient caves of mole, Redzepi had called together a team of superfriends. You may wonder, rightly, how a chef could presume to "comprehend" the cuisine of an entire country, such as Mexico, with its regional styles that shifted in nuance from village to village. Did Redzepi turn to cookbooks? No. His process was more hands-on than that. Like the head of an intelligence agency, he selected scouts to accompany him. His cooking depended on reconnaissance. He handpicked the scouts based on their aptitude for flavor location. Like Lord Baltimore, the Native American tracker in *Butch Cassidy and the Sundance Kid* who leads the search posse by recognizing patterns in hoofprints, cracked underbrush, threads of human scent, swirls of dust, and faint echoes of neighing in the canyon air, the Noma Avengers seemed to have highly honed antennae. They did not qualify, across the board, as experts on Mexican food. In fact, they seemed to have been chosen so that there was a sort of counterweight between expertise and beginner's mind. Rosio Sánchez and Santiago Lastra Rodriguez—for them, an understanding of Mexican food went all the way back to infancy. For Thomas Frebel, Mette Søberg, and Junichi Takahashi—from Germany, Denmark, and Japan, respectively—the ingredients of Mexico might as well have come from a distant moon.

Takahashi, who went by Jun and often accompanied me in the back of the van and who seemed capable of sinking into a somnambulist trance at any given moment, still couldn't handle the sear of a hot chile on his tongue. Nothing in Japan could compare to the wallop of serious spice he'd encounter regularly on the road in Mexico.

Søberg (the quietest of the bunch) and Frebel came with a European sensibility, yes, but their creativity seemed limitless. Frebel, whose carapace of chiseled muscle masked years of his youth spent in the pursuit of hard partying, told me that when he was a boy in East Germany during the Cold War, with little in the way of luxury at anyone's fingertips, an epiphany of flavor arrived in a box from the other side of the wall. In 1988 his mother was allowed to make a visit to West Germany, and she brought back with her a small assortment of mandarin oranges. Biting into the juicy citrus was, for Frebel, like pouring a flood of sunshine on the cinder-block gray of his East German surroundings. Was it any surprise, then, that as Noma Mexico unfolded, Frebel was often the first to greet the latest delivery of fruit from the jungles, all of it dripping with flavor?

Santiago Lastra Rodriguez was the fixer. It was up to him to lay down the groundwork before Redzepi and his fellow scouts came to town. His mission was simultaneously clear and impossible: find the best. The Best Ingredients. By any means necessary. Somewhere out there in Mexico awaited the best corn, the best epazote, the best octopus, the best escamoles, the best tiny bananas and young coconuts—Lastra Rodriguez just had to locate these delights and figure out how the Noma Mexico team could get access to them at the prime moment of ripeness and freshness. Sure. No problem.

Still in his twenties, Lastra Rodriguez had grown up in Cuernavaca, about ninety minutes south of Mexico City. Like many young chefs of his generation, he had come to a deeper understanding of cooking through the vehicle of the pop-up, that temporary mad-dash mode of food service that resembled a scavenger hunt crossed with an episode of *Top Chef* sponsored by Airbnb. Noma Mexico would be a pop-up, as had been its antecedents in Japan and Australia, but the Noma throwdowns had the depth of graduate dissertations compared to the average pop-up. Lastra Rodriguez liked to land in a place where tacos (and Mexican dishes in general) were exceedingly rare—Sweden, Italy, Taiwan, England, Russia—and find a way to cook them with the available ingredients. "It's a good way of exploring your culture," he told me. "You really miss that flavor. If you go to Russia, there are three hundred Mexicans in the whole country. No one knows what it is. When you see Mexican restaurants there, you don't want to go." For tortillas in Russia, he had relied on Armenian lavash. "Russia's very weird because they don't import anything," he said. In Moscow he had roasted shrimp with chipotle cream and stuffed it into the lavash with sauerkraut. That was the closest he could get.

If there were taco amateurs and acolytes here in the van winding around Mexico, Lastra Rodriguez could be counted among the latter. He was a student of the sauce dynamics and the counterpoints of texture and temperature that could make a taco sink or soar. Perhaps more important, his skill at navigating foreign marketplaces suggested that he had mastered the necessary hustle of finding the Best Ingredients regardless of obstacles. If the man had managed to make something close to tacos in Moscow, imagine what he could achieve in his home country.

"You see that billboard up there?" Redzepi said. "Straight ahead?"

The van was pulling into Zimatlán de Alvarez, a city near Oaxaca, and perched above the squat buildings with beaming maternal majesty was a photo of the chef Juana Amaya Hernandez, into whose orbit we were about to enter. All across Mexico there were young chefs bringing innovative twists and turns to the mysteries of mole, but if you wanted to journey into the depths of mole tradition, you would find no better a Virgil than Juana Amaya Hernandez. This was evident as soon as Redzepi and his posse stepped into the courtyard of Mi Tierra Linda, her restaurant and school in Zimatlán, where what she had set out for us looked like a museum devoted to the evolution of the chile.

"Wow," Redzepi said. "They're ready." Under a balcony, wood fires crackled in preparation for the parade of pots and pans that would, in intricate sequences of steps, usher us a bit closer to mole enlightenment. But the centerpiece of the display was a long wooden table with chiles of all colors and shapes laid out and labeled. Chile ancho and chile guajillo, chile de agua and chile chilcostle and chile onza—"This chile onza I've never heard of," Redzepi said—and chile chiltepe and chile solterito. Hernandez smiled sagely as Redzepi surveyed the smorgasbord of sweetness and heat.

Redzepi picked up a fruit called nanche and recognized it. "These need to be pickled, right?" he said. The discussion turned to escamoles, the white silky ant eggs harvested for a few days each spring. "It's like caviar for us," Hernandez said, with Lastra Rodriguez translating. The fact-finding mission seemed to be unfolding immediately. Redzepi was feeling ill, but he managed to mask that. I had never seen Redzepi sick in Mexico, but when I looked at him here in the courtyard in Zimatlán, I could tell. His skin had a greenish pallor. His energy had slowed, slurred—as if he were a wind-up soldier click-clacking to the end of its mechanical march. His face suggested that he had drunk too much of a liqueur called jaundice. He teetered, trying to hide his intestinal distress from his troops, but when he dashed away to the loo at Mi Tierra Linda for perhaps the seventh time, I knew something was up. Or down. (The reflexive ugly-American wisecrack about Mexico has always been "don't drink the water." It's a phrase that, like pearl-clutching warnings about "bad neighborhoods," tends to tell you more about the xenophobia of the person warning you than anything you need to be anxious about. I did not get sick in Mexico. I ate a lot of fruit and brushed my teeth with faucet water and never suffered anything more than a gentle loosening of the internal caverns.)

"I'm a little queasy," Redzepi told me.

Pain was shooting all the way into his joints. He was getting chills. His forehead had the clammy stickiness of the back side of Scotch tape. It was not an auspicious start to one of his research trips through Mexico with the team, and it was not the ideal condition in which to consume six or seven varieties of mole. He persisted anyway. Whenever he found himself in a situation like this one, with a respected expert at hand, he became like a five-year-old boy who can't stop repeating the question: *What's that? What's that? What's that?* You could almost watch the facts taking up residence in the absorptive encyclopedia of his brain.

There were at least two hundred moles in the Oaxaca area. The wood being used to heat up the comal was encino, or live oak. The frothy, porridge-like brew—it's called atole, and it was made with maize. "This is for breakfast?" he asked. "It's delicious. When you have it with the cold foam on top, it's like eating at El Bulli."

He took another sip. "But this is better," he said.

Redzepi had learned that the drink was pre-Hispanic; it was an echo of the era before the arrival of the conquistadors.

"What's that flavor? What is that flavor?"

Redzepi kept saying this to his team. He wanted to narrow it down. He wanted to eat a tortilla with nothing but salt so that he could follow its melody of flavor without interference. There it was—the chalky whisper of limestone, a residue of nixtamalization. "But it makes it more juicy," he observed.

He passed around an herb, a leaf. It looked like a fan held by a duchess enduring a heat wave. "Smell it," he said. "The hoja santa here . . ." Hernandez was serving a breakfast of beguiling simplicity: two tortillas with an egg in between them and a floppy green leaf of hoja santa. She pinched it closed like a dumpling.

"Do you like it?" she asked Redzepi.

"Yes," he said. "I'm learning. The leaves here are so powerful. The leaves here are very, very strong." He reached for a little ball of mozzarella-ish white cheese. "This is delicious. It has a little bit of the ferment, but that's nice."

There were conversations about the ubiquity of lard in

this region—"You can feel in the cuisine of Oaxaca the fat of the pork—a lot, a lot," Lastra Rodriguez said—and the Olmecan domestication of cacao, how the ancient priests used a cacao-chile brew as a ritual beverage. People from the Noma team took turns trying to puff up tortillas on the comal and grinding chocolate with the molcajete.

But . . . how would all these conversations and meals manifest themselves on a menu? "We have no clue yet," Redzepi said. "We are just absorbing everything."

There were more than flavors to absorb. There were sights, experiences, jolts to the system. Two days ago, north of Mexico City, they'd watched a lamb slaughtered for bar-bacoa. Days later they'd witnessed a volcano, Popocatépetl, casually exhaling puffs of smoke like a fat professor with a pipe. As we traveled along, we'd turn a corner and see a newlywed couple marching up a hill accompanied by a brass band. Now we piled into the back of a pickup truck and headed for some fields. The truck slowed down eventually, and we clambered out to survey stalks of sugarcane. A farmer waved his machete and cut some down.

"Sugarcane?" Redzepi said. "What's the season for sugarcane?"

"Right now," Lastra Rodriguez said.

"Have you ever been to Okinawa?" Junichi Takahashi asked me. "They have this—sugarcane." A chopped shaft of cane was passed around in case anyone wanted to gnaw on it. "Everybody's chewing on wood," Redzepi said. Then he spied something else. "Guys, that's wild lemon-grass here." It was overwhelming how much there was to learn. The history, the people. "Without that, you make food that's soulless," Lastra Rodriguez said. How the milpas, the traditional farms, had a trinity: corn, beans, and squash, all three of which worked together to nourish the soil and prevent moisture from wicking away in the dry air. There was the way the names of the chiles changed when they were dried and when they were pickled. There was the awareness of ingredients hiding within other ingredients, like the pixtle that came from inside the seeds of the mamey fruit and that played a role in the creation of tejate, the pre-Columbian quaff that Redzepi had drunk in the markets of Oaxaca. There were the detours of what-if speculation that took on the form of a jazz improvisation whenever a new flavor presented itself. This little yellow-orange bulb—what was it? Nispero, they were told—the Spanish word for loquat.

"How do you spell this?" Redzepi said, taking a nibble. "Nispero. This is an amazing fruit." It was sour, like a kumquat, and it had somehow made the journey from China to Mexico. "And you only eat the fruit? You don't eat the leaves?"

Thomas Frebel chimed in. "At one of those fancy restaurants in Oaxaca, do you think they have a dehydrator? Take the seed out. Dry it. It'd be the best raisin in the world."

All the fruits, all the chiles, all the nuts, all the herbs.

You could come to a knowledge of them individually, but even to brush up against the surface of the identity of

Mexico, even to pretend to get it, you'd have to make mole. It all came back to mole. Lightning wouldn't even threaten to strike unless the everythingness of mole could be meditated upon. Redzepi wasn't there yet. He was inching closer. He was like a monk sitting and waiting for enlightenment. On the preceding night the team had gone to bask in the presence of Celia Florian, another master of traditional moles. They had sampled eight of them—seven mother moles, the foundational pillars, as well as an insect mole with a formic base of chicatana ants. "Green mole to black mole to everything in between," Redzepi said, a trace of weariness in his voice—maybe the stomach bug was lurching back with force. There was a sense that the consumption of these moles had been inconclusive, ornamental—like looking at a vintage Mustang without having the opportunity to take it for a spin. "We have some ideas," he said. "Of course we will." *We will make our own.* This is where Juana Amaya Hernandez stepped in—proudly and forcefully. "Everything that you want to know"—she made it clear to Redzepi in Spanish—"*I know.*"

They'd make it from scratch. Chile chilhuacle negro and chile ancho are black to begin with, but they'd have to get blacker. The chiles were placed on the surface of the comal so that the heat could push them beyond darkness, beyond a mild scorch, into the heavy-metal realm of a starless night. "More burned," Redzepi was told in Spanish as he tried to grasp the distance he'd need to cook toward darkness. "More burned than this." A bottle of mezcal was opened, as if we would not be allowed to penetrate the Persephonic depths of gloom without a mind-altering intoxicant. The mezcal entered our bodies like a liquid key that unlocked our cellar doors.

Hernandez held in her hand a globe—a ball of mole base, a conglomeration of sesame seeds and almonds and raisins and garlic and onion and thyme and oregano and bananas and cinnamon and chocolate and pork fat and avocado leaf. The labor involved—"It's insane," Redzepi said. He wondered aloud: how much was necessary and how much signified little more than stubborn adherence to tradition? Young chefs around Mexico—Edgar Núñez at Sud777 in Mexico City, Jorge Vallejo at Quintonil in Mexico City, Francisco Ruano at Alcalde in Guadalajara, Angel Vázquez at Augurio in Puebla—were playing mix-and-match with the traditional recipes, taking mole in a range of new directions. Could the Noma team try to do something similar? To Takahashi, such an orgiastic paste of flavors was difficult to process. "I cannot taste what it is," he told me. "They're all mixed together and it's like a new taste."

Surrounding us in the patio kitchen were potted splashes of color: neon pinks and bruise blacks, rust browns and cactus greens: moles in motion. Redzepi peeled cacao pods and, taking turns with his Noma comrades, tried his hand at grinding them on the metate, a small stone table that required you to get on your knees if you wanted to make any progress. The stone rolling pin had to move forward at a distinct grinding angle to produce chalky globs of raw chocolate. It was hard work. It didn't produce much, when the Noma folks did it. Lastra Rodriguez's turn at the metate led to his athletically thumping the rolling pin over and over against the creamed cacao. "We've seen your sex face now," Redzepi said to him. "You know that, right?"

"Perfect," Lastra Rodriguez said with a sigh, looking at a feeble glob of cacao roughly the size of a pond frog. "We have one hundred grams."

"We have chocolate mousse for two," Redzepi cracked. "Can you imagine if we served people this—a home-made chocolate?" To make enough, men and women in the kitchen would be forced to grind it out all day and all night long. It would be worse than the clams in Japan. (For a single clam tart at Noma Japan, a tart topped with what looked like a briny tide of bonsai whitecaps, workers in the kitchen had to spend hours prying open freshwater clams with pins. "Too much labor had to go into each dish," Frebel said. "It was a group of ten people. Four hours in the morning, four hours in the evening." Just opening clams.) As Redzepi made this suggestion, I saw more than one of the Noma cooks visibly gulping. *Don't put it past him,* they surely thought.

Making mole promised to be no easy undertaking. "Before I came here, I had no idea," Takahashi said. Maybe the most elusive of the moles, the most complex and the most primally satisfying, was the black mole, which required some seven chiles and, under normal circumstances, weeks of study at Hernandez's elbow. "Es el Mexico," she said reverently. It was the peak, the underworld king of all moles. Could a European even dare to top a mole negro in its traditional form? "You can't," Redzepi said. "What you can have is new combinations—try to imagine a new textural delight within it. It's the same problem as in Japan. Once you start fiddling with something that has a very deep tradition, you very quickly look very stupid. That's when you get *mole foam*—just to do *something*." He shook his head as an indication of what he hoped he would not be stupid enough to succumb to.

The flavors had to sit together.

Spend time together. *Bind*.

For Redzepi, his thoughts about mole had to do the same thing. He autographed a wall at Mi Tierra Linda and posed for photos and said his farewells to Juana Amaya Hernandez and her crew. There were more places to visit, some of which had to do with a concurrent quest for the pottery, the tableware, that would ferry each Noma Mexico dish to each table. We dropped into a shop nearby and his disappointment was plain as day. "This is not the stuff I like at all," he said, surveying various plates. "It's too glazed. It looks like something from a shopping mall. It's not artisanal enough. I like it when things don't shout at you." In the van he admitted that he was coming down with chills and cold sweats, his bones and joints were aching. He felt weak. He'd eaten too much. He wanted to skip dinner. "Shall we just have a sit-down and go over the day quickly?" he asked the group. Thunder rumbled overhead. "Any of you have a rumble in the belly?"

———

This is how the conversations went in the van.

REDZEPI: To me the green moles—they're just like green sauces, in a way. It's a lot of ingredients in a sauce. [Pair them with jasmine rice and close your eyes and you might mistake a few of them for curries.] The black mole, for me—that's where the money is, man.

FREBEL: We can come up with very special, amazing moles. Our watercress purée is almost a mole.

REDZEPI: It's a mole.

FREBEL: I was saying to Mette and Jun, an insect mole would be amazing. [Cook it slow. Cook it for days.]

REDZEPI: I think burned coconut could be interesting as a fat. [He thought about that mole negro, its deep burn, its volcanic ash in the throat.]

SØBERG: The burned flavor was very pronounced.

REDZEPI: It's true the burned flavor was a bit much, although you wanted the chile flavor. [He was starting to understand something. Enrique Olvera's mole madre at Pujol in Mexico City had stunned him, perhaps induced temporary paralysis, but he was loosening up now.] I feel so much more comfortable after having seen this. You understand what it is—that there are many versions of it and you can do many things. It's up to you to mix it well. [Could a green mole be made with herbs? Leaves? Could the color come from unexpected sources?] If we could make it so silken . . . [A custardy tamale like a pike quenelle. Like panna cotta, but suffused with corn. Chilled sticks of jicama as a crudité. The pulp of prickly pear. But back to the matter at hand—time to focus.] Black mole. All right.

When the black mole is this intense, does it still work
with truffle?

SÁNCHEZ: Maybe not. [Sánchez usually said next to nothing
until the ripest moment, but then her insights regarding
flavor were invariably spot-on.]

REDZEPI: Maybe not.

FREBEL: They might cancel each other out. [Still, a tortilla
with truffle and black mole . . .]

SÁNCHEZ: Where did you have the burned coconut?

REDZEPI: I've never had it.

But he had an idea. He liked to understand things, and
maybe in that way he liked to control them, and right now
his understanding was locking into focus.

"I'm not afraid of mole anymore," he said.

Mérida

A S SOON AS MY PLANE LANDED IN MÉRIDA, I KNEW
something was amiss. I could feel it. I'd been longing to get back to the city and its crumbling postcolonial
beauty. I remembered the breakfast that Redzepi and I had
had the last time we were here in 2014: cochinita pibil in a
courtyard at the Casa Azul, one of the abandoned hacien-
das that had been restored to glory. I couldn't land a room
at the Casa Azul this time—the lovely family-owned ref-
uge was booked—so I found something cheap on Expedia.
After my flight landed, I gave a taxi driver the name and
address—the Boutique Mansíon Lavanda—and the taxi
began to inch toward the city in the middle of rush-hour
traffic. Along the way, my phone began to run out of juice.
I had about five minutes of power left on the phone when
the taxi pulled up alongside the hotel and the driver muttered an apology. The hotel was closed. Closed in the sense
that, at least for now, it no longer appeared to exist. The
building was gift-wrapped in the yellow tape you associate with crime scenes. Apparently the building had been
condemned. No explanation. No alert. No refund. I had nowhere to stay.

I owe it to Lauren that I scored one of the last available

beds in Mérida. There seemed to be some sort of conference going on. Preserving my remaining drops of phone power as if they were fresh water in the desert, I triangulated— while the patient driver waited for directions, Lauren, in New York, search engined her way from block to block in Mérida until she turned up a sole available room at a corporate megalith where the prices far outstripped my budget. She booked it just as my phone went dead. I should have seen it as a sign.

I met Redzepi and the Noma crew at La Rosita, across the street from Los Taquitos de PM, the al pastor shrine that had changed the chef's life years before. Right away I could tell that something was amiss here, too. Gloom flickered in Redzepi's eyes like fast-moving storm clouds. Roberto Solís was with him at the table, and what should have been the occasion for a toast—those first bites of al pastor had made Redzepi fall in love with Mexico years back—felt more like a premature wake.

"Our main partner pulled out," Redzepi said.

"When did you find out?" Solís asked.

"Two days ago," Redzepi said. "Big, big, big, big crisis." With a deep-pocketed patron pulling out, Noma Mexico's budget was now at least $600,000 in the red. The wealthy investor had gotten cold feet in the toxic churn that had followed Donald Trump's election to the American presidency a week or so earlier. He had originally promised to chip in a million dollars.

"In the thirteen years I've had Noma, I don't think I've ever been this stressed before," Redzepi went on. The team had planned to make a formal announcement about

the Tulum pop-up in a matter of days. A piece by Tejal
Rao in *The New York Times* was lined up to run, but the
Noma Mexico website wasn't up and running. Now Redzepi didn't know whether he'd have the money to cover the
event. It was too late to find another benefactor. "If we
raise the price, we're not going to be able to sell this," he
said. "We're very nervous." A number was starting to surface. Redzepi didn't like this number. He knew how the
number would be perceived—the optics of it. The number
was $600 per person. For dinner. In Mexico. "Just to break
even," he said. I watched him as he started stress-eating—
power-inhaling panuchos as if they were peanuts. "I've
had like nine of these," he said. "I'm so hungry."

His fingers drummed an invisible bongo. "Do you have
cigarettes?" he asked.

"No," Solís said.

"Of course it could be delayed," Redzepi mused aloud.
"This is the first time I know what stress feels like. We
are six months pregnant with this project. There's no
aborting it."

The next morning I walked from my corporate digs to the
small inn that the Noma reconnaissance squad had taken
over. I arrived to find Redzepi dangling from a tree—more
precisely, he and Frebel had found a way to hang gymnast's
rings from the branches of a tree in the inn's front lawn,
and Redzepi was using the rings to do pull-ups. He powered through his exercise routine and then marched over
to an outdoor table for breakfast. He rhapsodized about

the trips he and his colleagues had taken through Mexico. "We went to a town where they said 'If you take pictures here, people might kill you,'" he remembered.

"The grapefruit here is so much better than anywhere," he said. "I feel so good. A workout. Eggs and bacon. The sun is shining. Now if someone would just hand me a check for a million dollars, it would be the perfect morning."

At around lunchtime here in Mérida, Tejal Rao's piece would go live on the *New York Times*' site. "It's so nerve-racking," Redzepi said. "We need to find someplace to take some photos." Somehow the Noma Mexico site was prepared to launch. "Yeah, they've been up all night," he said. "The site says: 'You like tacos? Email.'"

"Minimalist," said Lastra Rodriguez.

Redzepi returned to being transfixed by breakfast. "Look at this fruit—is that dragonfruit?"

Like the spectral shuttering of my hotel, the loss of a seven-figure investor was but one of the surprises I encountered upon arriving in Mérida. Another was this: Redzepi and Sánchez and their lieutenants planned to cook a meal—sort of a trial run for Noma Mexico. The dinner hadn't received a whisper of notice in the stateside press. It would take place at Nectar, the restaurant where Solís still insisted on serving a trailblazing tasting menu in a city that didn't appear to have enough of an audience to support one. Much of the time leading up to the meal would be spent in marketplaces on a quest for the Best Ingredients. "They said 'You're gonna help us to find the best ingredients in

Mexico,' " said Lastra Rodriguez, upon whose shoulders
sat the task of tracking them down once again. "Okay. I
don't know what is the best. Then you find that they're
the things that are made with respect." To locate the Best
Ingredients you had to *understand* the Best Ingredients. A
shrimp that was still alive; an avocado that had just been
picked.

The challenge ahead would entail more than zero-
ing in on the Best Ingredients. It would mean securing
a consistent supply—in bulk, for weeks. With the Noma
Mexico announcement about to go viral online, Redzepi
seemed to be juggling several imagined glitches at once.
There were the critics who would howl about the ticket
price, and there were the critics who would take note if,
months later, Noma's $600-a-plate menu began to wobble
and derail because the Best Ingredients were stuck rotting
in a box three hundred miles away. Visibly on edge, he
and the group pulled into the offices of an organization in
Mérida that sought to support and protect Mayan artisans
and farmers throughout the Yucatán Peninsula. When we
walked in, we saw arrayed on a large table examples of
their wares: chiles, radishes, herbs, cobs of red and purple
and orange corn, pyramids of a local salt called espuma
de sal, and a dark watery honey, suggestive of vanilla, that
the Mayan people used for medicinal purposes. "It's from
the black bees, right?" Redzepi said, tasting a droplet of the
honey. "It's amazing." He took a whiff of a peppercorn that
gave off an aroma like a clove. He spoke to the people behind the organization with a warm but forceful directness.

"We've taken over a jungle site near Tulum where

we're going to build a restaurant," he told them. "Actually it's going to be announced in *The New York Times* in about ten minutes. We'll be serving five thousand people in two months. So if we want these ingredients, suddenly we'll need a lot of them." He paused, then continued. "So if we want to get these things, can we get a lot? We're coming here, almost ninety people, setting up lives. We've actually been to quite a few places in our inspiration journeys. We're trying to find the ingredients and be more inspired about how we cook. We're on the hunt for things like this that would inspire even Mexicans. Let's say we wanted eight thousand eggs over two months." He pointed to a bouquet of dried herb—wild oregano. "What if we wanted one hundred thousand of these?"

He was given the necessary reassurances. He was told that about three hundred and fifty Mayan families could provide the goods. It was this community, this network of subsistence milpas, that would receive much of the money being funneled into Tulum for Noma Mexico, but how could Redzepi explain that to the press without looking patronizingly magnanimous? Was there a right way to say it? The attack mobs of social media had made such utterances automatically perilous. Even when you were doing the right thing, someone was perched ready to ambush you on Twitter.

The *Times* story went live while Redzepi was tasting the honey. He was in the midst of telling me a story about how once, when he was sick, he had mixed the Mayan honey with some lime juice—and a spoonful or so had cured him.

I looked at my phone and saw the link. I told him.

"So it's out there," he said. "We hope for the best now."

He picked up a toy—a woven wicker replica of a sea turtle.

"Let's imagine," he said, "that we need five thousand of these."

The rest of the day Redzepi struck me as teetering on the edge of a breakdown.

It was not something I had ever witnessed. Around him there always hovered a bubble of composure. He usually seemed to be thinking three steps—or years—ahead of everyone else. To say that he favored control would be an understatement. All chefs are, to some degree, control freaks, meticulous with instructions, infuriated by careless deviations. Redzepi could not have powered Noma to fame without a hunger for control bordering on the fanatical. But he obviously liked to play with control, too—he liked to test it, the way a child learns to master the quantum chaos of a spinning top or a yo-yo at the tail of its leash. The pop-ups in Japan, Australia, and Mexico would stand as examples of this. He liked to blow up the Noma solar system so that he could race like hell to wrestle its planets back into a new alignment.

This time, Redzepi could not be sure that he could restore the orbit. This realization was written on his face. On the way to the market he murmured about what the servers would wear at Noma Mexico. "I don't want a group of very, very white Northern Europeans looking like a circus act in Mexican clothes," he said. He seemed to be analyzing the optics of every gesture, but he was worried that one false move would ruin the whole endeavor. He and the Noma cohort hit the Mérida market like agents in a *Mission: Impossible* movie. The best way to stop worrying was to get to work—to cook.

"Right now the idea is that we select ingredients that we want," he said. "So what do we want?"

"Do we want the pumpkin?" Mette Søberg asked.

"Yes," Redzepi said. "Pumpkin. Calabaza. Also the lime that tastes like bergamot. We'll see how the urchins are. When they come in. *If* they come in. Should we do a taco?" Apparently there wasn't a menu yet for the Noma dinner the next day.

"Maybe with the octopus," Rosio Sánchez said.

"We have the clams from Nayarit," Santiago Lastra Rodriguez chimed in.

"The clams," Redzepi said. "They might go well with the white beans."

They were planning dinner on the fly. "This is very spontaneous," Redzepi told me. "Sometimes it's okay to be more spontaneous." Was he trying to convince himself? He found a seat and tried to jot down the order of the dishes:

> *scallop mole*
> *clams and beans*
> *avocado tamal*
> *sea urchin*

"Okay," he said. "Let's try to write the menu. What should we start with? I mean, we don't really know if it's

gonna work. It's just a plan. We'll see what happens. Let's
see if the urchins come in. Let's see if they taste good."

His mind was not really on the menu. The menu would
take care of itself. His mind was in his fingers and his fingers were fidgeting with his phone and his phone wasn't
getting a clear signal. Service here in the Mayan world
could be spotty at best.

I mentioned a news email I had just received. It said,
"The Zika virus is no longer a global emergency." This was
another one of Redzepi's growing concerns. Zika had been
tearing through the Caribbean, embedded in mosquitoes
and tied to awful birth defects in babies born throughout
the region. Many of Noma's workers were in the prime
of their childbearing years. Persuading them to venture
into a veritable hot zone posed an ethical risk that no one
wanted to tangle with. "I've followed the Zika alerts," he
told me with a sigh of relief. "I was so nervous about it."

At the moment, though, he was nervous about the whole
enchilada. The news about Noma Mexico had, thanks to the
Times, entered the mediaverse, the terrordome of Twitter,
but . . . he couldn't access it. Response had slowed to a crawl.
Was the price putting people off? Would Zika anxiety sink
the ship before it even had a chance to set sail? Redzepi was
hearing from back home in Copenhagen. At the equivalent
of this stage in the process—after the news had broken—
Noma Australia had already been fully booked, with a
waiting list numbering in the thousands. Noma Mexico . . .
the enrollment . . . gulp . . . so far was a trickle . . .

"If it doesn't work out, Noma's bankrupt," Redzepi told
me. He had already taken on a huge burden of risk by

closing down the original location in Denmark. "I'm very, very, very, very nervous. For the first time, it's a make-or-break year for Noma. It's all amazing stuff. We just don't have enough money to do all of it." He looked at his phone again. He wanted to know how many people had touched base with the site about Noma Mexico.

"It's a lot less," he murmured. "It's alarming. People are not signing up."

How many had the Sydney pop-up attracted this early out of the gate?

He gulped. "Thousands."

There are those days when nothing seems to be going right and the only cure just might be a heap of al pastor tacos. Redzepi and his team crowded around a table on the edge of the Mérida marketplace to wait for platefuls of the finger food that had kick-started Redzepi's love affair in the first place. But the fire wasn't burning. A few yards away, the trompo—the spinning spit on which the pork for al pastor tacos slowly cooks in a live flame—had conked out. "I think the trompo broke." Redzepi sighed. "It's pastor tartare."

Roberto Solís, who apparently had operative phone service, optimistically announced that he had spotted some online item about Noma Mexico.

"Don't retweet that," Redzepi said. "They'll just make fun of us. And it's all about the price."

His temper was fraying. His nerve endings jangled like a hundred invisible car alarms. Everything grated on him.

He saw a mother on the outskirts of the marketplace furiously slapping her daughter.

"I got beaten so often as a kid that I could never imagine doing it to my own kids," he murmured. He looked at the team. "Vamos," he said weakly. Into the crowded aisles of the marketplace. Into the crush. How often had he gone searching through these aromatic mazes? He delivered instructions: "Two kilos of caviar." He was joking. But he did want that lime, the one that smelled like bergamot. He checked his email again. Jay Cheshes, a food writer, already wanted to do a piece for the *Wall Street Journal*. Redzepi checked the Noma site again. About two hundred people had registered. A shudder of phantom pain passed over him. He suddenly looked a decade older. He grabbed lime after lime. He brought lime after lime to his nostrils. He needed the fucking lime that smelled like Earl Grey tea. Where was it? He was Ahab and the white whale was the lime that bore the odor of bergamot. How could you find it?

"Get lucky," he said.

They sped off to the kitchen of a culinary school to test the flavor combinations.

Pretty soon the room turned into a chamber filled with tear gas. Rosio Sánchez was roasting chiles for a mole negro and the stinging vapors began attacking our eyes and lungs. Not that this dissuaded her. "Wild Horses" by the Rolling Stones started loping out of her phone. "Too soft," she said. She switched the soundtrack to "Paint It Black."

Blackness hovered over the proceedings. The Noma crew got to work with the silent industry of astronauts who had but a few minutes to take soil samples from a previously unexplored planet. The Copenhagen office had gone to bed, so Redzepi was forced to sit tight for the next round of updates. "Everybody's sleeping back home, so that's really annoying," he said. "Let's see how this whole thing is going to go down. Hopefully the public is not going to slaughter us. I wish we could've charged $250. Our dream was that we would get help from the government." There were plans in place to fly ninety people round-trip from Denmark to Mexico—the travel cost for that alone would tally up to hundreds of thousands of dollars. Noma would rent out an entire apartment complex in the urban precinct of Tulum. International currency rates were in flux. The American election seemed to have thrown everything into chaos. "Every time the dollar drops, income drops for us," Redzepi said. "I need another cigarette. I'm so stressed." He stepped outside of the kitchen with Thomas Frebel.

"Are people only going to talk about how this is too expensive?" he asked.

"No," Frebel said.

"I am worried," Redzepi went on. "We've had so many setbacks on this. It has been so much harder to do this than the others." Second guesses swarmed in his head. Should they have selected Oaxaca instead of Tulum? Oaxaca was being paralyzed by strikes and protests. "The week before we were there, we couldn't have entered Oaxaca," he said. What if they'd chosen Oaxaca for a $600-per-person pop-up—only to see the city shut down by political strife?

The blackness was a moveable feast. They carried it with them to Nectar, where they were scheduled to sit for a tasting menu prepared by Solís and his kitchen. The signature dish at Nectar was an onion encased in the powdered blackness of ash. Biting into this onion produced a collision of smokiness and sweetness and cream—the interior cradled a marble of mayonnaise. I ate several of these deliciously char-brushed onions. Redzepi could barely get one down. "I have, like, no appetite," he said.

Midway through the meal he cleared his throat and summoned a huddle at the table. "Okay, guys," he said with forceful dejectedness. "I need to speak with you. Because I'm kind of half depressed right now." He mentioned the coverage online—the tweets, aswarm in the mediaverse like taunting hornets, only getting angrier if you tried to swat them away. "We're getting a lot of criticism. A lot. So I need to know what you guys think. How stupid does it make us look?"

"I think if people know why it costs that much, they will understand," Søberg said.

"I will be honest about it, of course," Redzepi said. But had the damage been done? "I guess what I need you to answer is, *Did we fuck up?*"

The thing about Redzepi and his cult was that everything locked into place, everything hummed in harmonic convergence, whenever they blocked out the noise and got back to the food. The aha moments constituted more than menu items that customers would enjoy. They were points of contact, portals of cognitive breakthrough. And so it was that Redzepi began to regain his equilibrium in Mérida at approximately the same moment that Rosio Sánchez had the epiphany of the two sauces. This was the cosmic mole insight that would confirm to everyone who tasted it that a fuckup could be averted—and in fact converted into something new and old and weird and beautiful. In the kitchen at Nectar, hours before the dinner, Sánchez took the mole negro that she had been brewing the day before and mixed it up with dollops of the funky caramel-hued scallop fudge that they'd brought along from the Noma mothership in Copenhagen.

The result was a revelation, causing a click of delight on the palate.

Redzepi tasted it on a spatula and stopped in his tracks. "Now I think that's amazing," he said. "This is incredible. Oh man oh man oh man. This is the perfect mix of the two places. Maybe here we have a dish for Noma Mexico." He high-fived Sánchez and Frebel. It was hard to tell whether the ambient spiciness in the air from the chiles had made his eyes watery. "This mole is a masterpiece."

The food helped. Being in the kitchen helped. Being surrounded by his talented associates helped. "I'm more calm today about this experience," Redzepi said. "If we don't sell this one out, then we don't sell it out. We'll come up with a different plan. That's how we do things. But I do think we'll sell out." The fog of sniping and stinging on Twitter—it eventually evaporates if you wait long enough.

"Honestly, it's making me think these people are dumb," he said. "The press is a horrible beast. The press is like an angry head chef."

Watching from the margins the whole time was Roberto Solís, whose laid-back stoicism seemed to make Redzepi relax and bristle in equal measure. It was a symptom of Redzepi's Danish conditioning that he wanted everything to fall neatly into place; it was a truth at the core of Solís's understanding of the world—of Mexico, in particular—that he knew such a thing was impossible. The Twitter storm about the price?

"I knew that something like that was going to happen," Solís said with priestly resignation. Why?

"Because Mexico is a poor country," he said. Teaching a Scandinavian to adapt to Mexico's go-with-the-flow rhythms? Well, that could take a while. It was a process. It was hard to tell whether Redzepi was attempting to impose order on Mexico or whether it was the other way around. The day before, Redzepi had berated his old friend over the phone about not having enough plates on hand for the dinner at Nectar.

"This is kind of what Mexico is," Solís said. You need plates. You wait for plates. The plates come or they don't. You have a plan A and a plan B but also plans C, D, and E. A plan Z wouldn't hurt, as backup.

"Once you understand this, you can laugh at it," Solís said. "But you have to suffer first."

———

In the afterglow of the dinner at Nectar—a jubilant occasion that had ended with mariachis serenading the guests and a cart stationed outside serving up a "dessert" of al pastor tacos for anyone who wanted to punctuate the night with the postparty snack of the gods—I had not expected to encounter the Branding Man.

I saw him when I wandered over to the Noma team's inn in the morning. The Branding Man was cooler than you'd expect, which is to say he was conscious of his role as an ambassador of corporate lucre and so he carried himself in such a way that any underlying douchiness would be imperceptible. From the way he was dressed—Coachella casual, with an unbuttoned shirt and a tasteful menagerie of tattoos—I might've taken him for a rival journalist or a young Mexican chef whose membership in the cult of René Redzepi had remained heretofore unknown to me. When I heard him talking, though, I realized that the Branding Man, whose first name was Alfonso, did not cook or write. He had a different agenda. "If we can agree on that, we can sell it to brands very, very easily," he was saying. I could not tell what he wanted the Noma crew to agree on, but I could tell by the look on Redzepi's face that it pained him to contemplate such a concordance.

Redzepi and his band were huddled around the Branding Man at the breakfast table. The visitor represented a new way forward—a solution, you might say, to the pesky problem of having an investor rescind a sizable percentage of Noma Mexico's proposed operating budget. Noma Mexico couldn't happen in a vacuum. It wasn't just going to *materialize*. Like an art installation or a touring band, it needed an infusion of capital in order to come together. As the emissary from a massive international spirits conglomerate, the Branding Man could ostensibly make that money (and more!) reappear with the snap of his fingers—if only, that is, Noma Mexico might be open to a few inventive accommodations.

"We want to make some special products for the brand," the visitor said. There was an inviting vagueness, a dip-your-toe-in-the-pool conversational warmth. What would a win-win scenario look like? Well, let's say a signature cocktail at the Noma Mexico bar—using one of the conglomerate's popular tequilas. (Mads Kleppe, the beverage guru at Noma, had been scouring the country for months looking for the rarest, weirdest, most obscurely artisanal mezcals. I could only imagine the look in his eyes, the basset-hound droop of his jowls, if he were instructed to whip up a strawberry margarita as a way to appease some corporate sponsors.) Let yourself dream. How about a sponsored video?

Grabbing a seat at the table, I silently imagined a corporate logo burned with an actual branding iron into one of Noma Mexico's young coconuts. But no, the Branding Man was not an idiot. He knew not to overreach. He clearly had a sense of where Redzepi's priorities lay. An idea had surfaced—maybe the conglomerate could help subsidize a school. "We'll have many things happening around the project," he said. This is what made it tempting. You could solve your financial problems in one stroke while also doing some good for the local community. Win-win-win.

And yet all of this represented alien territory for Redzepi.

"I'll be very honest with you," he said. His voice was measured and calm. "I'm not a big fan of working with brands." For thirteen years or so, Noma had managed to avoid any corporate ties. Once Coca-Cola had offered Noma $500,000 just to put up a couple of recipes on the Noma site—recipes that would somehow involve soda, an ingredient as far removed from the ethos of Noma as Manhattan is from Manitoba. Redzepi turned that down—at a moment when Noma was, frankly, desperate for cash flow.

"We have to charge six hundred dollars because we have no sponsors," Redzepi went on. "Who the fuck knows what could happen—and something *will* happen. If there's a happy medium, it would be amazing. This thing with the schools is fucking sick."

The Branding Man detected receptivity. "Making things happen," he said with enticing open-endedness. "Without the brands we can't do the schools. With the brands we can do ten schools. Brands—they have the money. And they are going to continue existing in the world whether we like it or not. My head is spinning right now." He smiled and left the possibilities floating in the air like dust motes.

Redzepi's head was spinning, too—for different reasons. The night at Nectar had gotten a little wild as it unraveled. Multiple mezcal shots had marked the crossing of the finish line, and the fiesta had left toxic vapor trails in Redzepi's skull. (This was rare. Most of the times I was around him, Redzepi politely hovered at the rim of a wineglass without imbibing much. Beyond a sip here and there, he did not seem to delight in it. Although it's not difficult to surmise that displeasure arose from the risk of surrendering control.)

"Today my workout was getting out of bed," Santiago Lastra Rodriguez said.

"To have such a night—when will we recuperate from this?" Redzepi said as they boarded a van to take them into the jungle. "I really feel like shit, I have to say. Does anybody have some aspirin?" Being René Redzepi, he pointed out that real aspirin came from the bark of a tree. "It's foraging."

The van went silent. Fingertips squeezed temples. There was a lot of thinking to do. There were questions about the purpose of the mission and the problems that come with forging alliances with organizations whose aims are not the same as yours. There were the challenges of trying to mount something that would be greeted as a tribute to the people and cultures of Mexico as opposed to some craven neocolonialist sleight of hand. There were the issues of intention that could be encapsulated in works such as Teju Cole's piercing essay "The White-Savior Industrial Complex" in which he had written about Africa but could also have been writing about Mexico and the whole Caribbean region:

> One song we hear too often is the one in which Africa serves as a backdrop for white fantasies of conquest and heroism. From the colonial project to Out of Africa to The Constant Gardener and Kony 2012, Africa has provided a space onto which white egos can conveniently

be projected. It is a liberated space in which the usual
rules do not apply: a nobody from America or Europe
can go to Africa and become a godlike savior or, at
the very least, have his or her emotional needs satis-
fied. Many have done it under the banner of "making
a difference."

There was the desire to do the right thing, to make
a difference, yes, but in the political climate of 2016 and
2017 there were ever-evolving definitions of what doing
the right thing looked like. There was perhaps a need to
reconnect with something essential—a need to remember
what this whole Noma Mexico enterprise was supposed to
accomplish and celebrate in the first place—and so it was
fortuitous that Redzepi and his comrades were riding out
toward what he would later describe as one of the three
best meals of his life. (The other two were prepared by
his father and his wife, respectively, in ascending order of
closeness to his heart.) We were rolling to Yaxunah, a village down a dirt road. We were, less precisely, taking a trip
to a hole in the ground.

Of course, Redzepi's madeleine moment with Mexican
food had happened years earlier in the form of tacos al pastor, courtesy of that late-night, streetside initiation provided
by Roberto Solís. If al pastor qualified as the "Jumpin' Jack
Flash," a snort of carnal abandon compressed into a bite
or three, cochinita pibil delivered something deeper and
heavier—cochinita pibil was the subterranean operatic
sweep of *Exile on Main St.* Like that Rolling Stones epic,
cochinita pibil gave off the odor of dirt. That's not a meta-

phor. After all, how could you get closer to the abundance of the earth than a wild pig cooked *in* the earth—its meat buried in a hole, fragrantly entombed in a steam chamber of banana leaves, perfumed with sour orange that had sprouted out of the same soil? "*Pib* is the Mayan word for the traditional oven, or pit barbecue, of the Yucatán Peninsula and it is still used in the villages today," Diana Kennedy writes in her 2000 book, *The Essential Cuisines of Mexico*.

> *It is prepared by digging a rectangular pit about 2 feet deep. The bottom is lined with large stones that are heated with a wood fire. When the embers have died down and the stones are considered hot enough (only the experts know this by instinct) the meats to be cooked—pig, turkey, or meat pies like Muk-bil Pollo—are wrapped in several layers of banana leaves, set in a metal container, and covered with sacking and earth. The cooking takes several hours. Meats cooked this way have a very special flavor and succulence.*

We wouldn't have to wait for the succulence. The drive out to the village was long enough that it coincided with the slow collapse into deliciousness of the meat. "They say the cochinita is ready," Santiago announced as our van got close to Yaxunah, where the habitations had thatched roofs and lizards posed frozen on windowsills (until darting away) and wild turkeys strutted around the yard. "In a lot of these Mayan villages—alcohol is forbidden. Because it drives them crazy," Redzepi said, perhaps himself susceptible to a similar line of thinking after a morning of squinting agony.

There may be no more effective hangover cure than an excursion to Yaxunah. The men wore straw cowboy hats and outfits of white; the women had red flowers woven into their hair and embroidered ones on their dresses. The women sat on the ground pounding masa into tortillas; the men stood around and astride a smoking pit.

"Where's the pig?" Redzepi asked.

"The pig is here," Solís said, motioning toward the smoke drifting upward from a covered area that looked like a pile of leaves. "Don't walk here."

Surrounding us were trees. "Can you ask what kind of citrus this is?" Redzepi said. "Those leaves are amazing." The full circle of cochinita pibil rose around us: sour orange and achiote trees—ingredients directly at hand.

"They're gonna open it," Redzepi said. He sounded like he was talking about rolling back the stone that blocked the entrance to Christ's tomb. Maybe he wasn't far off. The men began to go at the pit with shovels. They removed dirt, blankets, fronds, and sticks. Then, carefully, they hoisted out a big metal pot that had been at rest on red embers. The men opened the pot. An aroma as seductive and complex as that of a cassoulet or a doenjang jjigae flooded the air. It was the scent of melted fat and meat that had broken down slowly, tenderly, like a rock split by ice crystals. "Oh, it smells amazing," Redzepi said. "Ask them about the banana leaf—does it add flavor?"

The meat was escorted with care to a table near the women, who had by now shifted into tortilla-crisping

mode. Tasks in many Mayan villages, and throughout
Mexico, tend to be segregated according to gender. Men
here were prohibited from touching the masa as it made its
progression toward tortillaness. Women were the experts,
and were rightly revered for this. Redzepi stood by the
comal as the women laid the dough on it. He studied the
process as the tortillas formed—in their ideal manifesta-
tion they would puff up, the development that still seemed
to elude the greatest chef on the planet. "There we go,"
he said as a tortilla inflated as if taking in the breath of a
hungry ghost. "This is Yoda-level tortilla making. Oh, I'm
so ready to eat."

Suddenly Redzepi had an idea. "We should ask them
what they're doing in April and May." He meant the
women who were placing one perfect tortilla after another
in baskets. What if . . . ?

Redzepi filled a tortilla with cochinita pibil, which had
been shredded off the bones of the pig and was marinating like a stew in its own juices. He placed pink pickled
onions on top. He took a bite. He closed his eyes. The meat
was juicy and shot through with layers of spice and citrus
and fat. The tortilla was thick, chewy, redolent of corn—as
with a good bagel, a good tortilla expressed its character
through its density and depth of flavor instead of coming
across like some gummy, generic conduit for supermarket
flour.

Redzepi looked me in the eyes. "Have you ever had a
better tortilla than this?" he asked me.

I had not. He nodded slowly. He was coming to a
decision.

"We made an arrangement to get all the corn from this community for the pop-up," he went on. But it was clear that he now felt as though he had to take things a step further. "Roberto?" he said. "Can you ask them what they're doing in April and May?"

A few months later the result of his decision was on full display in between the dining room and the kitchen at the pop-up in Tulum. Redzepi had bid the Branding Man farewell, but he had invited the women of Yaxunah to join the team at Noma Mexico.

Redzepi had that Ken Kesey–ish sense of the pilgrimage. He understood the fuel that comes from theatrical gestures. He knew how to inspire his team. And so it was that the communion with the cochinita pibil was followed by a trip deeper into the past. Our van was headed for the ruins of Chichen Itza, where Mayan and Toltec cultures had collided and merged and built grand, mystical structures more than a thousand years ago. He wanted everyone to see the pyramid—the Temple of Kukulkan, also known as El Castillo.

But our arrival at this temple of antiquity gave us a shock at first. Clustered thickly around the perimeter of the site was a whistling, chattering bazaar of souvenir stands—tables where local people sold T-shirts and toys. Mayan tchotchke hawkers seemed to be holding bongs up to their lips, but it turned out the bongs were something that a Foley artist might use in a movie: they were toys that, when blown into, would emit tropical bird whoops and jaguar roars. These sounds surrounded us as we walked toward the pyramid. Once we'd passed through the commercial scrum, though, we came upon the ruins rising from a grassy expanse. "Understand the enormity of the town that this was," Redzepi intoned, echoing Shelley's "Ozymandias" as he had us pause and gaze upon what had once been glories. "Look how amazing this is. They used the cosmos as their guiding compass. There are so many layers to how they built it and why they built it." The pyramid had been designed so that twice a year, during the spring equinox and its equivalent in the fall, the setting sun would create playing serpentine shadows that made it look like a snake slithered down the steps of the edifice.

We wandered into a stadium. It was more than five hundred feet long and had once been the site of Mayan ball games. "See the rings?" Redzepi said, relishing the role of tour guide. "Those were the goals for the Mayan games." The acoustics of the stadium were said to be so sophisticated that you could shout into the temple stationed at one end of the ball court—known, aptly, as the Temple of the Bearded Man—and the sound would carry across the field to be heard with perfect clarity at the other end, bounced like a rubber ball from one stone wall to another. "So they could communicate with one another like that," Redzepi said. We decided to test it. Rosio Sánchez aimed her voice at the Temple of the Bearded Man and shouted.

"Hola!"

The echo boomeranged to the other side of the playing field as if it were being broadcast on stereo speakers, and it was, at that moment, possible to imagine a conversation between the creative dreamers of the present moment and their counterparts centuries earlier.

We spent the night in the magic city of Valladolíd. No joke, that was its official designation. It had been deemed, by the government, one of dozens of Pueblos Mágicos, chosen for their innate delightfulness. What it lacked in culinary dynamism it made up for in charm. The streets were so quiet at night that as you strolled down them you could overhear conversations through the windows, and the twin steeples of the Iglesia de San Servacio glowed with golden light.

The next morning we were back in the van, where reality and magic were yet again at war. If Redzepi simply left his phone off, he could keep the hounds of reality at bay. He could marinate in the sleepy analog reality of a morning in Valladolíd. But a few movements of his fingers activated the device and instantly he saw an email from Ryan Sutton, a critic at *Eater*, the influential food blog, asking some hard questions about the proposed price of the meal in Tulum. (In media circles, Sutton was known as the grumpy uncle of American food criticism, such was his sensible but ultimately buzzkillish fixation on How Much Everything Costs, Damn It.) This was why Redzepi had known he could never have his first Noma pop-up take place in Mexico, even though Mexico, more than Japan or Australia, was the country that fired up his imagination. He knew the optics were a problem. He had to plant seeds first.

"Oh, man, I could have a pile of those tortillas from yesterday," Redzepi murmured in the van as he contemplated how to respond to the *Eater* query. "And that broth—oh, please take me back there, take me back." I could never be entirely sure, while riding shotgun in the Noma express, what was in store for any given day. Redzepi, like a military general, planned everything down to the last tank advancement, but he often declined (or just forgot) to disclose the plans to me until the definitive moment was at hand. What I knew was that we were simultaneously going forward and back—back, this time, to the place where I'd found myself sprawled on the beach before dawn, flashlight rays in my squinting eyes and sand in my teeth. We were going back to Tulum. We seemed to be doing so with hellhounds on our trail. There was the negative media attention being trained on the cost of a meal at Noma Mexico. "You can't make expensive tacos," Redzepi mused, still gnawing on the conundrum of the price. "So how do you do that? The bottom line of all this is that our expenses are so big. That's what I'm trying to say. It's an impossible thing." Meanwhile he had his eye on the hellhound of death. Toggling among emails and texts and links on his phone, he learned that his close friend the British writer A. A. Gill had been diagnosed with cancer. Actually "an embarrassment of cancer," as Gill would write in the U.K.'s *Sunday Times*. "There is barely a morsel of offal not included. I have a trucker's gut-buster, gimpy, malevolent, meaty malignancy." (Gill died about three weeks later. It was the first of several deaths that shook Redzepi in the years to come.) All of this tumult was putting Redzepi in a philosophical frame of mind. He sat in the van and stared out the window at the acres and acres of jungle thickets.

"I'm much more relaxed about it now," he finally said of the pop-up. "It's gonna be what it's gonna be."

What it won't be is like the pop-up Noma in Tokyo. "We're not going to put ourselves in a situation like that in Japan ever again," Redzepi said. "Never again." In Japan, the Noma team had needed extra labor, but the labor force kept getting chipped away by mandatory quarantines at the Mandarin Oriental hotel where the pop-up took place. If anyone in the kitchen tested positive for the norovirus, that person—and that person's roommate—had to stay out of the kitchen for three days, which created a round-robin cycle of absences. One challenge after another made the Tokyo residency too arduous, too much of a grind, whereas the Sydney pop-up had been, for someone of Redzepi's temperament, almost too easy. "At the end I couldn't wait to get out of Australia," Redzepi said. (This could be viewed as a bizarre assessment when you consider what the journalist Tienlon Ho had written about the crises and snags on the dock in Barangaroo: "There had been a few headaches. They had arrived to a restaurant half-built at an address that didn't yet exist online. Sinks weren't working. Neither was the oven. A box of expensive ingredients had disappeared, and storms ripping across Tasmania meant more orders wouldn't get through. Two leafy nests of *gulgulk* [green ants] from the north arrived in one box, and it was evident from the carnage that boundary disputes had devolved to warfare; the formic acid behind the ants' ferocity and tangy coriander-lemongrass-kaffir-lime flavor was completely spent.")

Redzepi wanted the Tulum pop-up to land somewhere in

between Tokyo and Sydney: to be difficult enough to push everyone without crushing their spirits. "This is a process of our becoming confident and finding ourselves," he said.

The scent of grapefruit filled the van. Junichi Takahashi sat toward the back, flipping through a Japanese/Spanish dictionary. Tapping away on his phone, Santiago Lastra Rodriguez stayed on the lookout for a cenote—one of the wild lakes that dot the Yucatán, formed when the asteroid crashed into the peninsula and pockmarked the landscape with pond-sized pellets. Redzepi wanted to visit a grand cenote, a true cenote, not one of the touristy ones. The cenote of his dreams was like the Mayan octopus of his dreams and the cochinita pibil of his dreams and the Faroe Island langoustines of his dreams and the Norwegian mahogany clams of his dreams. "If you had a machete," he said in the van, "and you went a kilometer into the jungle, you might find one. One where you have more of that nature contact."

We enter Tulum. We're back.

"There he is!" Redzepi says.

The van slows down along the shady, sand-strewn road that parallels the beach. This road is like some matchaganja hipster fever dream. Sandals, seawater-tangled hair, yoga arms, towels wrapped sarong-like around slow-moving hips, a dazed parade of Savasana-stoned human beings drifting to wherever. "Many American people," Takahashi observes. One of the drifters is familiar. The van stops and the door opens and James Spreadbury climbs in. "How the feck are ya?" he says. Our global unit now has a representative from Australia.

Spreadbury and his family have been encamped here for weeks, laying the organizational groundwork for the pop-up. The van moves forward slowly until we get to a modest clearing across the street from La Zebra. "Look to the right, guys, because you're gonna be seeing our new restaurant," Redzepi says.

The site amounts to little more than an abandoned back lot. As with the location of Noma 2.0 in Copenhagen, which was cratered with cement and masked with graffiti, this patch of real estate looks a long way from rehabilitation. The air smells like mango juice and cigarette smoke. There are random piles of white rocks. The floor is dirt. "This is the kitchen," Redzepi says, gesturing toward some dumpsters. "Hard to imagine, huh?" You could say that. He pantomimes the act of expediting dishes. "Pick up! Table two!" There are no tables yet, though, and no roof, and no walls, and no stoves, and no sinks. "It's very different than what we've done otherwise, guys," he goes on. In Sydney and Tokyo, the pop-ups came together at established commercial properties; there was infrastructure in place. There were bathrooms. This—apparently the followers of Redzepi, like the followers of Joseph Smith in the desert scrub of Utah, were being instructed to build something out of nothing in the wilderness. And like the early Mormons, the Nomatics weren't troubled by the slightest twinge of hesitation. "What do you think, Thomas?" Redzepi asks.

"Amazing," Frebel says, his eyes aglow.

"We're keeping all the trees, right?" Mette Søberg asks.

"As many as possible," Redzepi says.

"It's so cool," she says.

"It's so cool," he agrees. "What do you think, Jun?"

"Here we can do something special," Takahashi replies.

Then Redzepi turns silently to the one who often seems like the hardest to impress.

"Everybody will be happy here," Rosio Sánchez says.

There is the panic when you realize you've lost your wallet. The panic when you think someone is illegally buying things with your credit card. The panic of your phone conking out precisely when you are trying to locate one of your children in a busy, dicey part of town. The panic of learning that someone has hacked into your social media account and begun sending scurrilous messages to your friends and colleagues. In spite of—or because of—a torrent of technological advancements, our civilization seems to have multiplied the number of opportunities for things to break. There are days when our lives amount to a blur, a feverish hopscotching from one glitch to the next—trying to fix things in order to stay put as opposed to trying to create things to move forward. The more gadgets you have, the more often they crack or go dead; the more desperately you depend on them, the more desperately you freak out when they fail you. A sense of purpose erodes, replaced by a sense of being aboard a sinking ship that is always springing new leaks that you have to patch up. Meanwhile larger fissures and fractures develop. The euphoria and comfort of love are replaced by the tedium and tetchiness of putting out fires. Your marriage is falling apart. Your profession is falling apart. Your country is falling apart. Your government is hurtling toward fascism and your world is careening toward environmental doom and you'd love to pay more attention to that, really you would, but you just dropped your fucking phone into the garbage disposal.

For anyone who has ever imagined a different way, an alternative mode of occupying the earth in which every action was the fruit of some higher purpose, a few days spent in the company of Team Noma could feel positively ambrosial. Surely there was no shortage of problems. Every day delivered a fresh batch of snafus along with the foraged berries and edible insects. But the glow of some ultimate goal gave everything that sense of meaning that felt so comparatively elusive in the crushing grind of trying to stay afloat and serene in twenty-first-century America. To watch the Noma crew at work was to come to understand why otherwise intelligent people join religious cults. It's not for the free love and cathartic dancing, although those early enticements have their appeal. It's because a cult tells you: *We have the answer.* Without an answer, even a manufactured one, life is a slog. With an answer, there is a unity of purpose that can focus the mind and energize the body.

The purpose, now, was pulling off Noma Mexico. Years of planning and dreaming had gone into it. Making it happen had almost driven Redzepi mad. But there was no turning away. This had to work. One false move and the whole thing could capsize.

Tulum

René is never happy with where he is at.

—MATT ORLANDO, chef, as quoted in the *Wall Street Journal,*
November 5, 2014

ET'S GO SEE SOME TURTLES," REDZEPI ANNOUNCES.
He's sitting at a long table with friends and family members at El Pez, the hotel in Tulum where he has camped out for the duration of Noma Mexico. Laid out on the table is a spread of local fruit—papayas and watermelons, mangos and mameys—as well as sunny-side-up eggs and tortillas and spicy green salsa and slices of avocado. Today is a day off, and he has packed the schedule with activities that should ostensibly be stress-relieving. We convene for yoga under a thatched roof in a hut that's raised up on stilts; a breeze coming off the Caribbean cools us down. Then we pile into a van to go to a beach at Akumal to float among the ancient chelonians.

The van has a screen at the front, behind the driver, and Nadine switches on *Finding Dory* for the three Redzepi daughters. Nemo's dad appears on screen, voiced by Albert

Brooks, representing in all his neurotic anxiety the very antithesis of Nadine and René when it comes to parenting styles. "The only reason to travel in the first place is so you don't have to travel ever again," the father fish warbles. It's safe to say the Redzepi family sees things differently.

On the drive out, Redzepi is uncharacteristically silent. At this point I have traveled to Mexico with him numerous times, and I'm used to his hopped-up pontifications—the electric current that seems to race through his system whenever he encounters an unfamiliar ingredient or custom. But now he is strangely muted. The van arrives at the turtle beach and Redzepi becomes every beleaguered suburban dad in history, hovering impatiently on the curb waiting for everyone to get equipped with towels and sandals and beach chairs. The slow crawl of the children disembarking from the van seems to drive him to distraction. "It's your day off and you spend half of it waiting around for people to get their shit together," he mutters. Pretty soon it's like a Chevy Chase movie. Everyone's kitted out in masks and snorkels and bulky life vests whose straps scrape against your skin. Wading into the water is the opposite of the cold shock of the ocean that many of us are accustomed to. The water is hot. Not merely warm, but heated up in a way that makes you worry about everything from flesh-eating microbes to catastrophic climate change. We bob around in the Mexican bathwater and come to the realization that the turtles are farther out than we are—out where the water gets deeper. The turtles are, in fact, a few yards beyond a line of rope. You can see their shapes in motion, their heads surfacing now and then, but anyone who swims under the rope gets snapped at by megaphone-wielding officials who are monitoring the beach.

Redzepi will have none of it. The frustration that has clouded him all day seems ready to burst into thunder. Someone mumbles something about it being against the law to venture beyond the rope. "Fuck this shit," Redzepi says finally. "Let's just do it." And with that call to arms he leads us. One by one we slide under the rope and head en masse for the open water where the turtles cavort in a slow aquatic ballet.

Each morning the Noma Mexico kitchen sputters slowly to life. First the fires are lit—logs and sticks roaring into redness and spitting sparks from the ovens onto the stone floor. Cooks arrive in waves and, after spraying their ankles with mosquito repellent, get to work at their stations. Paulina Carreno and Mariel Nogueron, both from Guadalajara, are deep-frying masa in vats of oil. There are pans of fresh wet kelp from the Sea of Cortez, tubs of beach mustard and sea purslane and saltwort from the shoreline not far away. Fejsal Demiraj, a cook who grew up in Yonkers, New York, chops raw meat with a knife—or so it seems. Upon closer inspection you notice that what looks like "meat" is actually local tomatoes whose red pulp flirts with purple. He checks out a delivery of tomatoes in a box. They are already rotting, some of them moldy and glistening and collapsing. Demiraj knows he has to improvise—to use fewer tomatoes, only the intact ones. The good tomatoes—Indios grown in a local Mayan community—will have their seeds and skins removed before they are dried for a few hours in a dehydrator to concentrate the flavor and convert their texture into a pleasurable leatheriness. Then he will brush them with chile de arbol oil and chop them down to be tucked into salbutes.

A few steps away Junichi Takahashi scrapes the seeds out of a heap of habanero chiles. Perhaps he has a gift for nimbleness that winds up burdening him with the most tedious of dishes. This one is both tedious and perilous. The seeds harbor invisible agony. Takahashi has to be careful about where his fingers go. He scratches an itch on his neck. "Oh, fuck, it burns!" he yelps.

Eggs are boiling, tomatoes are charring directly on the coals, seaweed is shifting from rust-brown to flaming chartreuse in hot water. Transformations are happening in the heat. It's a circus of funk and char and tang. Everyone's wearing sandals and black shorts and gray aprons—the uniform lends the kitchen an air of military precision. But the dishes being assembled exemplify all meanings of the word "wild." They are wild in their integration of the flavors and textures of the untamed—it's a menu that highlights ant eggs and grasshoppers—while at the same time they are wildly inventive. (In one, you squirt a spritz of michelada directly into your mouth using a bulb of floating kelp as your shot glass.) The wildness is wired into the structure. "When it's really windy, you can listen to this palm tree, the way it's moving in the ceiling," Frebel tells me, nodding toward a trunk that rises right from the

center of the kitchen. "You can't have that in Copenhagen—to be exposed to the forces of nature." You might say
that Noma Mexico is more Noma than Noma itself. "The
first thing René told me is, 'Thomas, we need a tree in our
kitchen.'" Strung along the posts holding up the ceiling
are the skulls of pigs.

A laminated chart on the wall provides information
for anyone who hasn't internalized it yet. "Wild food from
the jungle," it says, above a splash of images of moringa,
caimito, hoja santa, piñuela, grosella, flor de mayo, wild
royal, wild lentils, maiz pibinal. A chart of herbs features
sea purslane, sea lily, saltwort, beach mustard. When Santiago Lastra Rodriguez arrives, it usually means that some
of these ingredients have arrived with him as their escort.
He's the fixer, the stocker of the supply larder, logging
hours from 5 A.M. to 2 A.M. in a byzantine web of contacts
with scores of producers and purveyors around Mexico. "I
drove like five thousand kilometers in one week," he tells
me. "Monday I was feeling so weird because I had a few
hours off. I got, like, freaked. I freaked out completely. I
was just standing thinking, 'What's going on?'"

Frebel picks up a jackfruit—it looks like a spiny
football—that has arrived with the latest delivery. "It's
not ready yet," he says. "Touch it. You want it softer. When
it's ripe it's like the best honey." He grabs a machete and
chops it open. The jungles surrounding Noma Mexico are
full of such fruits, but that doesn't mean they're easy to
secure. "We always have some troubles," Lastra Rodriguez says. "You never know, when you wake up, what is
going to happen." During the first week of Noma Mexico,

he needed a supply of piñuelas for the opening bite of the meal—a fruity nub of bromeliad bud sheathed in tamarind paste and cilantro flowers. Lastra Rodriguez was contacted by the man growing them. "He sends me a selfie at like six in the morning: 'The jungle is on fire.'" There was a brushfire. The farmer's land was being incinerated. Lastra Rodriguez needed to find an alternative source. "So I had to drive around asking people in the community. You drive two hours and you ask for Juan. You go there and you ask, 'Where is Juan?' They say, 'Juan is in church.'" The hunt goes on and somehow, after six hours of driving around looking for Juan, Lastra Rodriguez comes back to the Noma Mexico kitchen with a crate of piñuelas. "What took you so long?" someone asks him.

The octopus comes from Campeche, but Lastra Rodriguez cannot reveal precisely where. "There're just a few people who know where to get this octopus," he says. The fisherman told him, *I need a boat, an engine, three days of work a week, and a dependable supply of mezcal.* Deal. "No restaurant in the country can get fresh cacao fruits three times a week. It's just impossible," Lastra Rodriguez says. So how did Noma Mexico luck out? "We did a deal with a guy," he says. The convoluted route of produce in Mexico often ends up robbing it of its ripeness. Picked in the peninsula, produce will sometimes pass through Cancún, get hauled all the way to Mexico City, then boomerang back around to the Yucatán. By then it's dead. "You never know what you're getting here," Lastra Rodriguez says. His goal, then, is to procure the Best Ingredients directly from the people growing them. "We get this stuff fast," he says.

Sometimes they go even closer to the source—all the way to the seeds. Redzepi and his team wanted to use Indio tomatoes. "It is a tomato that is impossible to find," Lastra Rodriguez says. So they found amateur farmers. "We gave them the seeds, they planted them, and they are growing them behind their houses." Eventually the first crop of tomatoes arrived at the Noma kitchen. They were full of worms. Lastra Rodriguez had to go back to the growers to talk about the need for speed when it comes to picking tomatoes in a jungle climate. "You just work with them, work with them," he says. "It's not always simple for the community to understand the quality we want." Still, now, some tomatoes arrive already rotten.

The escamoles—ant eggs—come from Hidalgo. There the delicate eggs are harvested and frozen. "If they defrost, we are fucked," Lastra Rodriguez says. One shipment of escamoles was due to land by plane in Cancún, but a storm kept the plane from touching down. The escamoles were diverted to Mérida, hours away, at 8 P.M. He could only contemplate what condition they'd be in.

There is a doctor on call in case anyone conks out in the 100 percent humidity; the Scandinavians in the crew are not accustomed to it. "Last week we got a B-complex shot," Frebel says. "Just to make sure everyone stays healthy." My eyes must look glazed, because he interrupts a young cook who's got his head down in prepping a dish: "Get Jeff a glass of coconut milk." Chilled containers of coconut elixir— sweet, cold, nutrient-packed—are at hand all day long.

Sour oranges, tiny bananas, calabazas, mamey seeds whose cores are pressed into oil. Everything needs to be converted rapidly into its gastronomic ideal. Decomposition lurks for anything left in limbo. "We would have saved them for Thomas Keller, but we're serving them to you," a cook tells me, gesturing toward the dwarf bananas.

Redzepi arrives in the kitchen. "Any sandwiches left?" he asks.

His voice is not the commanding bark of a martinet. He asserts his dominance more diplomatically than that these days. There is a liquidy ebb and flow to the way he talks that seems to bury a question in each sentence. He leads by suggestion. Today's staff lunch is a pile of sandwiches stuffed with cochinita pibil. Redzepi is not one to stuff his face mindlessly, not even with a delectable torta. He picks up a sandwich and places it right on the hot grill to toast it up. He doesn't appear to take much pleasure in this. The restlessness of the sea turtle expedition has only thickened like the quick-spreading mold on those jungle tomatoes. He has come to Mexico for years with an elusive objective: to relax and escape the oppressive gray dome of a Copenhagen winter. So why is it that here in the equatorial swelter of his beloved Tulum he has his mind fixated only on . . . Scandinavia?

"By next week," he tells me in a mumbled rush, "we're going to start going into Copenhagen mode. We have to." David Zilber, Noma's director of fermentation, sits at a table a few feet away, conspicuously separate from the boiling and chopping of the kitchen. He has his laptop open and has trained his focus on the wild fermentations afloat back in Denmark. In fact, he's writing a book about them, a collaboration with Redzepi that will arrive in 2018.

In a kitchen overpopulated with deep thinkers, Zilber stands apart. Fortune favors the bold, et cetera: Zilber had for years worked as a relatively unknown cook in Vancouver, but he got hired by Team Noma out of the blue after emailing an impassioned essay to three restaurants that he viewed as representing the vanguard in global cooking: Saison in San Francisco, Alinea in Chicago, and Noma in Copenhagen. The first two never responded. "I always say, if you're not uncomfortable, you're not pushing yourself," Zilber later told the writer Nikita Richardson, more or less encapsulating the core truth of the Noma gospel. "So I sent out just a handful of résumés and a really long cover letter

to my favorite restaurants." Around the kitchen in Denmark he became known as the "walking Wikipedia."
Even a casual conversation with Zilber was likely to swerve
its way into references to mathematics, history, quantum
physics, biology, chemistry, and cinema. Redzepi had
moved him from the kitchen to the fermentation lab,
working alongside Arielle Johnson and Lars Williams,
after Zilber had managed to turn an episode of Saturday
Night Projects into a philosophical experiment. Instead of
merely devising a new dish, Zilber came up with a series
of boxes. The boxes, with their strategically placed blind
partitions, would foster a conversation in which each diner
at a table at Noma would experience a different version of
a dish using the same ingredients: red mullet with beach
herbs, black olive, and potato. (In one case the mullet
would be a mousse, in another a fillet, in another a tartare,
and in the last sashimi.) Zilber called this risky entry into
the Saturday Night Projects spectacle "Ruminations on
Solipsism Along a Mediterranean Coastline (De Gustibus
Non Est Disputandem) Variations 1–4." He accompanied
the "dish" with an essay, from which here is a sample:

> *One serious question many cognitive scientists ponder
> is that of the nature of experience itself. The ways in
> which light manifests itself to different individuals, your
> threshold for pleasure, your perception of taste. These are
> very real mysteries of the human brain. There's a classic
> stoner's conundrum. It goes by the name of the color in-
> congruency test. It's the idea that though we might both,
> you and I, recognise the color of an eggplant to be purple,*

that outside of our consensus on the matter, we can never
really know if we're both, indiscriminately, experiencing
the SAME purple. For all I know, purple to you might
be what I call green.

Redzepi took notice.

Now Zilber, like the avatar of one of his own metaphysical tracts, is physically present in Mexico but mentally elsewhere—in Copenhagen in the future. "I have to think a year in advance," he says. Menus that will be mapped out for 2018 are already on his mind—and on Redzepi's.

Thomas Keller is flying into Noma Mexico for dinner on Saturday. Demand for extra tables is boiling over: The other day a rich woman was spied along the perimeter of the Noma Mexico tableau, tossing hundred-dollar bills through the gate and begging for a seat. A Tom Sietsema piece in *The Washington Post* has come out; its headline refers to Noma Mexico as "the meal of the decade." Redzepi doesn't celebrate. He can't seem to stand still. After all of the searching and labor and torment that he poured into turning Noma Mexico into a reality, he seems curiously unable to enjoy the way it has settled into success. And here's the thing about food. You taste it and it's gone. Whether or not Redzepi qualifies as an artist, his chosen medium is one in which the most impressive creations evaporate from view within seconds of being witnessed. You pick a mango. You suck the juice out of the mango. You finish off the sweet remnants of the mango. You're left with the pit. You plant the pit. If you're lucky, you get to watch the pit sprout into bloom and the cycle shudders back to its stations. Redzepi's food is not simply a communion with nature. His very approach to the restaurant —the rhythms of create-and-destroy, bloom-and-decay—can be viewed as an ode to nature itself. In keeping with those rhythms, Redzepi isn't comfortable with stasis; he's allergic to inertia. If something isn't in motion, in transit, he's bored with it—or maybe in that situation he's simply bored with himself. "René keeps saying 'the beast is tamed, the beast is tamed,'" Frebel tells me. "The thing is, it's going well here. Getting here was more challenging than the other ones"—in Japan and in Australia—"but in terms of execution, it's by far the easiest one."

And easy—easy doesn't fuel Redzepi's engines. Here in Tulum, the moment is upon him. Night after night, he and the kitchen team go through the complicated steps of an intricate ballet. But as the choreographer, he remains distant. He's engaged, but his mind is elsewhere. It is Redzepi's assistant, Devin McGonigle, who gives me a glimpse of what, after years on the road with the guy, I've come to accept as his driving force. I'm standing at the bar and watching the Noma troupe rehearsing in the kitchen. With Redzepi, McGonigle tells me, "there is no now." There is only the propulsion you see at Saturday Night Projects, at a marketplace in Oaxaca, at the old, original Noma when Redzepi decided that the time had come to abandon it. McGonigle tells me that there is one sentence that she hears over and over when Redzepi is speaking with her. The sentence is "Can we move on now?"

Epilogue

THIS MUST BE THE PLACE

Copenhagen

I believe what we're cooking here and now at Noma is ultimately something that comes from within; reverberations from long ago, rather than a cerebral construction. Looking back at the last six months, the best moments have happened when something in the present connects with stories from the past. "What is creativity?" I've been asking myself while writing this journal. I'm not sure, but tonight I will answer it like this: creativity is the ability to store the special moments, big or small, that occur throughout your life, then being able to see how they connect to the moment you're in. When past and present merge, something new happens.

—RENÉ REDZEPI, *Journal*

IN ALL OF MY VISITS TO COPENHAGEN I HAD FAILED to notice it: Copenhagen was a fairy-tale city, an ice-cream cone of a city, the place that gave us Hans Christian Andersen and his stories, the place that had inspired none other than Walt Disney to build a joy factory. My visits to Denmark had always been Noma-centric, concentrated on the culinary nerve center of the metropolis, but on the last of my trips I happened to take along my twelve-year-old son, Toby, and we got on bicycles and I saw the city with new eyes—or older eyes. On the Monday after Easter the sun came out. Toby and I made a beeline for Tivoli Gardens, the amusement park full of roller coasters and bumper cars and peacocks and ruddy-cheeked children in various stages of glee. It was during several visits to Tivoli starting in 1951 that Uncle Walt, then known as a producer of films, nurtured the idea that would evolve into Disneyland.

Toby and I wavered, at first, when we spied the Star Flyer from afar. It looked like a whirligig that a giant had hoisted in the air after impaling screaming human beings on protruding spikes. Uncovered seats, carrying people who were snapped into orbit with nothing more than a rudimentary steel bar, rose rapidly into the air and then spun around and around like dogs on a leash. We almost balked, but with coaxing from a Tivoli employee who spoke English in tones of gentle chiding, we decided to go for the ride.

The trip with Toby had a sweet undercurrent. Back home in New York, during the month after our traveling together in Denmark, Toby and his sister, Margot, would greet the arrival of their twin brothers, Jasper and Wesley. Spending a week in Copenhagen, just the two of us, was a way for Toby and me to savor the calm before that peculiar storm. The foundations of my life had collapsed and re-formed in the four years since Redzepi had first met me for coffee in downtown Manhattan. It may be one of the lesser-known insights from Ecclesiastes, but apparently there is a time for blowing everything up and a time for building it all back. Now I hovered a few weeks away from becoming a father of four. Early in January, Lauren and I had signed some papers inside the Spanish-style courthouse in Santa Barbara and had stepped outside to get married by a justice of the peace in the California sunlight that we'd always associate with home. A ukulele duo played "Maybe I'm Amazed" and "Sea of Love." It was a small wedding. Our guests were our two sets of parents and Lauren's brother, Danny, who'd managed to fly into Santa Barbara from Los Angeles in a tiny prop plane. Danny had to do that because a lethal mudslide had wiped out entire neighborhoods in Santa Barbara County and had flooded Highway 101 with rocks and mud and debris. There was no direct route to drive from Los Angeles to Santa Barbara; a drive that would usually take a couple of hours now required about six hours of curving east and heading north through the Central Valley before slicing westward toward Santa Maria. Danny preferred to fly. In spite of the small-and-fast nature of our nuptials, Lauren and I had wound up exchanging our vows in front of an audience of one hundred or so schoolchildren. They watched us silently and ate their noontime sandwiches. We were told that they had congregated there, on the lawn behind the courthouse, because the mudslides had shut down their school.

While I had been home, Redzepi had been averting his own disasters. The risks that he had initiated years earlier, driven by his hunger for change, had come close to wiping out whatever he had built. Noma 2.0 had opened, but barely, and the month when I was getting married in

Santa Barbara might've qualified as the worst month of the chef's life. "Owing to the property's historic significance and Denmark's strict landmark regulations, construction was bound by rules Redzepi only discovered after they broke ground," wrote Howie Kahn in a report about the restaurant's shaky resurrection.

At one point last summer, construction came to a halt when parts of a 17th-century wall were unearthed. Preservationists were called in to determine its significance. "They told me it could possibly take two years to figure out what it was and how it might affect us," Redzepi says. "I couldn't sleep, couldn't breathe. We would have gone bankrupt." This doomsday scenario was averted. "They finished their evaluation after five weeks," Redzepi says. The delay did set the restaurant's opening back by more than a month, becoming another unforeseen event in a series that at times left Redzepi feeling he should have never initiated the move. "It's been insane," he says. "But there are just things you say yes to, even before you know how to totally plan."

Toby and I met Redzepi and his family for brunch at Sanchez. If anyone thought that Redzepi's hunger for Mexican food could be sated by a few months in Tulum, they were mistaken. He craved it more than ever. Rosio Sánchez, now presiding over her own full-service restaurant, knew to keep a long table set aside for the Redzepi family on Sunday mornings: Nadine and René, Arwen and Genta and Ro, Nadine's mother, Bente Svendsen, and her sister,

Berrit. Sunday was a restorative day for Redzepi, the previous week of service having careened to a close with Saturday Night Projects. Salsa and masa provided the needed sustenance. Tostadas topped with smoked salmon, oysters whose cavities had turned tangerine with a mignonette of sea buckthorn and habanero, fresh warm tortillas ready to be rolled around pockets of eggs and carnitas. The restlessness of my last encounter with Redzepi, in Tulum, had been replaced by something else. The buildup toward the grand opening of Noma 2.0 had been tumultuous—Nadine compared it to the gut-churning anxieties of the norovirus crisis in 2013. At night, sleep needed to be coaxed. Redzepi would toss and turn with worry. At the bottom of the struggle, when construction of the new Noma was delayed for two months because of the discovery of those old stones in the dirt, Redzepi had succumbed to sleeping pills in order to force his body into a state of rest. Now he depended on something else. At Sanchez, to show me, he pinched his fingers to his lips, pantomiming a puff on a joint.

If he kept moving, he didn't have to think about it. In moments of repose, it came back to him, the way he had spent his fortieth birthday in a hospice in Copenhagen, sitting by his father's bedside, watching cancer get the final word. His father had died four days later.

"Forty-five years ago, my father came to Denmark as an Albanian Muslim immigrant," Redzepi wrote in an Instagram post on December 22, 2017. "Like many others before and after him, he spent much of his life in an adopted country, toiling as a manual laborer, cleaning dishes, hauling fish, driving taxis, cleaning floors. A lifetime of double shifts. My father took comfort in cooking a good meal, and the pleasures of family around a table, eating and sharing. I remember waking up in the morning, the smell of burning wood, seeing my father tending the fireplace, hearing the crackling sound of chestnuts roasting for breakfast. His tomato salad, sliced wafer thin, with a dash of vinegar and a fistful of sweet parsley leaves. The bean stew. The sauté of spicy sausage and onions . . . those are only memories now. Everything he did was to bestow his family with happiness and better opportunities. Never once in his life did he complain, not even when the cancer ate him from within. Every success I have found in my life, I can connect to a sacrifice he made."

In a city that had inspired Walt Disney to erect a replica of the Matterhorn on a flat expanse of Anaheim, California, Redzepi had fashioned his own version of Tomorrowland, Adventureland, and Fantasyland. He had rebuilt the city in his own image, redrawing the old maps, changing the way Denmark talked about its own cuisine. Gloom would overtake him, especially on those days when the pain of his father's absence was at its most acute, but he could keep moving and he could keep gathering with his family for tacos. He watched the table at Sanchez and smiled as plates of food were passed around and shared. "I feel like I'm eating sunshine," Nadine said.

As the new Noma debuted with a seafood-dominated menu, Redzepi posted stories on his Instagram feed that were titled Failures1 and Failures2. These were gastro-

nomic gaffes so odd that they bordered on the comic, and he tapped into their humorous potential in his captions, but the irony is that at Noma it could be hard to tell the difference between the dishes that made the final cut and those that didn't.

"Smokey cod face broth. Is the eye too much? (It does have a purpose.)"

"This is a fish bladder—you can eat it, buuuuut we don't really know."

"That time we tied two octopuses together to make 'pancetta'. . . . NOOOPE."

"Hermit crabs got released back into the ocean."

" 'Pickled squid' never really worked."

It said something about Noma—and the appetite for risk that was embedded in the international pop-ups and Saturday Night Projects—that Redzepi didn't hesitate to air his R&D mistakes in public. And it said something about Noma that those mistakes didn't come across as being worlds away from the delights that customers would be rapturously Instagramming a few days later. To dust off a famous quip from *This Is Spinal Tap*, it's a fine line between clever and stupid. It's a fine line, too, between delicious and disgusting. The constant push forward would yield far more duds than hits. Noma was like a band that had tasked itself with writing a new song every day, just to see what would happen, and there were some fans of the band, like David Chang, who stubbornly insisted that the early songs would never be surpassed.

One morning during my week in Copenhagen, the Momofuku chef and his wife, Grace Seo, ambled into the Redzepis' kitchen, where Chang began to wax nostalgic for Noma in its leaner and hungrier years, its us-against-the-world years, when Redzepi himself (in league with core comrades like Matt Orlando and Christian Puglisi and Lars Williams) had dreamed up the first series of Noma classics by marrying a distinct geographical philosophy to force of will.

The musk ox tartare, Chang mentioned.

"Oh, I loved that dish," Nadine Redzepi said.

The langoustine on a hot rock, Chang said.

"I loved that dish," she said again.

Unlike songs, these dishes could not be heard again. You couldn't download them or stream them. Maybe someday, if Noma were to announce its closure, Redzepi would resurrect them for a last stroll down memory lane, but it was difficult to imagine it. Redzepi in temperament appeared to mirror the natural world from which he drew inspiration. Nature was nothing if not a symphony of flux. "Rather than taming nature, as farms tend to do, the new Noma would let it in," Lisa Abend wrote of the new space. Nature would govern it, too. The menu, the team, the purpose of each room would only change and change again.

The new Noma, when I got to it on foot, did not look remotely finished, and that felt right. Parts of the property were still walled off behind plywood. The original Noma sign, ceremoniously removed letter by letter while a crowd watched at Strandgade 93, didn't appear to be back up yet. As far as I could tell, there was no sign. There was no grand entrance. There was no way to figure out where the front door was. *Welcome to the new Noma*, which could easily have passed for a Humboldt County pot farm. "A week before the restaurant was to open, a massive tarp protected the still-exposed space from rain and snow, the lounge windows had yet to be installed, and the dining room ceiling wasn't complete," Abend wrote. "The staff had long abandoned the idea of landscaping. Special projects director Annika de Las Heras was just hoping they'd have time to throw some mulch over the thick mud that surrounded the restaurant. Cooks and waiters worked through the night, hauling planks and stuffing acoustic insulation between the ceiling slats. And that was before the kitchen tops failed to appear."

Maybe all of the delays and glitches had forced Redzepi to reel in some of the grand sweep of his dreaming. As I approached the perimeter of the new Noma with Toby in tow, I couldn't help but recall my bumpy ride to the site two years earlier, in a wooden bicycle basket that would normally have carried a couple of kids or the day's haul of groceries. From the outside now, the view wasn't that different. Brambly foliage sprouted out of a bunkerish mound. Half-sunken houseboats bobbed on brackish water. In the distance, right across the border of Christiania, you could see one of the residences of that anarchic precinct. It looked like a teepee.

Apparently the Noma bakery was up and running, and Mette Søberg (now even more of a creative force at the restaurant) could be seen conducting flavor experiments behind the glass of the R&D chamber, but other areas of the compound—was this a greenhouse? was that an ant farm?—were still under construction. For a diner in the spring of 2018, the effect was that of experiencing a work

in progress. I suppose Noma always existed as a work in progress, shedding skin and evolving from one larval form to another from year to year, but the mud-tracked, makeshift quality of the setting conveyed the feeling of a Broadway musical that was still working out a few kinks in previews.

Inside, though, it was a different story. Ali Sonko and Bente Svendsen greeted us with hugs at the entrance, and we were led through the front door. Inside was clockwork. The kitchen looked familiar—it turned out that Redzepi had used the outdoor kitchen at Noma Mexico in Tulum as a model, a beta version, of the kitchen his crew would put into action here in Copenhagen. It was a long, commodious space punctuated by islands, at intervals, where squads attended to specific dishes with practice-it-ten-thousand-times precision.

"It is the season of the birch water," a server told me and my lunch guest, who happened to be Pete Wells from the *Times*. Even our drinking water here at lunch would carry a trace of the forest. Birch trees had been tapped for their woodsy elixir. What followed that sip was a feast both refined and barbaric, with juicy brains sucked out of shrimp heads and clam butter scooped into your mouth with the rim of a Venus clam shell, blue mussels arranged like wings and plumply nestled in pools of kelp butter. There were mahogany clams from the Faroe Islands and scallops that Roddie Sloan had hoisted from the sea bottom in Norway, their cool flesh served with a bright orange melting cube of scallop roe in the shell. Sea snails and roses, cloudberries and pinecones—the arc of the meal amounted to a strange chamber music of popping and melting, explosions of sweetness and brine, the contours of oceanic flavors. Sea snail and sea urchin and sea cucumber—once again Redzepi was like Glenn Gould doing the Goldberg Variations, reimagining the intricate counterpoint of Bach, or in this case the ocean, with a hundred different shifts in tempo and tone, stressing this note over that, cooling, heating, isolating, overlapping, juxtaposing, seeing what the vastness of the ocean might be capable of when placed into human hands.

When I had the sea urchin dish, in which rows of glistening pumpkin seeds stood at attention nestled closely together like a cartoon church choir or a nest full of hungry baby birds, I couldn't help but eat it and rewind to the journey I had been on for four years. Here was uni as cloud light as a soufflé, its tangy froth married to the nutty chew of the seeds. The Noma menu was constantly new, chronically in transition, but here I detected a link to the past. There was an echo, in this dish, of the dish at the original Noma that had first sent me drifting away. Maybe it was because of that dish that I had gone off on this spree, boarding spur-of-the-moment flights and emptying my pockets as some kind of self-medication. To eat a bite so perfect that it calls you to sell your house and join the circus—absurdly but undeniably, that was the impact that that sea urchin had had on me. This new dish of uni got me looking back at the miles I'd traversed and the calories I'd consumed.

Keep moving. It's the only way. That was the "lesson," if there was one. I may've been caught in a momentary loop

of Proustian flashback reels because of that uni, but Redzepi himself was already moving forward again, just as he
had been in Mexico and Australia. "Look at these ducks,"
he told me as we wandered out around the lake after lunch
had ended. "I can't wait to come out here and shoot some
for the fall menu."

He was kidding, I think, even though it's true that Noma's fall menu would focus on the funky delights of wild
game. He wasn't kidding about the bear. "Last year we
were offered five bears," he said. "From Sweden. We might
take one of them. Young bears are tasty bears." Right now
all of the fish tanks in one of the Noma compound's eleven
chambers held live crustaceans and shellfish, each tank
carefully calibrated to stay at the temperature and salin-
ity level most appealing to each particular sea creature.
But come autumn, after the close of the summer vegeta-
ble menu, it would become a game room. There would be
birds and beasts hanging and aging in the wild air. The
flesh would age and be transformed. The air would turn it
into something else.

Thomas Frebel was gone now. A core member of the
Noma A-team, one day he had announced that he was moving to Japan to open his own Noma-influenced restaurant,
Inua, and that was that. Malcolm Livingston was gone,
too. He had parted ways with the restaurant after the cur-
tain fell on the original location, moved back home to New
York, and teamed up with the Bronx-based Ghetto Gas-
tro collective to cook and travel around the world. Back in
New York, Danny Bowien had closed Mission Cantina—his
attempted mastery of the tortilla never having clicked—

and reopened Mission Chinese Food in a new Chinatown space, personally evolving along the way into a gym rat and a cheekily insouciant style icon. Enrique Olvera had opened two successful restaurants in New York City, Cosme and Atla; Pete Wells had named Cosme the best new restaurant in New York in 2015. Redzepi's wife, Nadine, had published a cookbook called *Downtime*. Daniel Humm's Eleven Madison Park had topped the 50 Best Restaurants list in 2017, and Massimo Bottura's Osteria Francescana had followed at the top the next year. In both years, 2017 and 2018, Noma had been out of contention because of Redzepi's mission to reinvent the whole enterprise. There was bound to be news in the spring of 2019, when Noma would be back in the game for good.

In another room next door, here in Copenhagen, David Zilber was experimenting with the changes wrought by time and air. "Peaso"—miso made with peas—lined Zilber's shelves in various fermentation permutations. "You can't see that last drop that goes into the mussel," Redzepi said. "But that drop is like ten years in the works." Time— that was the secret ingredient at Noma. Time would pass, and everything would change, and more would be learned, and people would come and people would go, and stuff would break and stuff would get fixed, and everything would inch closer and closer to some new frontier of deliciousness.

"We believe this is our future," he went on. "Fourteen years of trial and error—you start to know things." Even the rooms themselves would move forward—they'd be adapted to new uses with each passing season and each new flood tide of ideas.

"We're in here for life," Redzepi said, waving his arms as if they could measure the expanse of this new home. "But we're not in here for one thing. It can change. It can change. It can change."

Acknowledgments

THANK YOU to these people, without whom I would've remained lost on that beach:

Lauren Fonda
Anna Lipin
Steve Diamond
Scott Waxman
Ashley Lopez
Timothy Hodler
Gabe Ulla
Amy and John Risley
Steffi and Curt Gordinier
Susan and Richard
    Gordinier
Margot, Toby, Jasper, and
    Wesley Gordinier
Judy and Peter Fonda
Lisa Abend
Jay Fielden
Michael Hainey
Kevin Sintumuang
Helene Rubinstein
John Kenney
Stephen Satterfield

Ian Daly
Melina Shannon-DiPietro
Nadine Levy Redzepi
David Chang
Alejandro Ruíz
Omar Mamoon
Daniel Patterson
Pete Wells
Phyllis Grant
Adam Sachs
Jason Tesauro
DeLauné Michel
Tom Junod
Fabienne and Jeremy Toback
Rosie Schaap
Peter Tittiger
Arve Podsada Krognes
Annika de Las Heras
Katherine Bont
Lau Richter
Ali Sonko

Dan Peres
Jesse Ashlock
Deborah Needleman
Whitney Vargas
Sam Sifton
Patrick Farrell
Emily Weinstein
Tiina Loite
Carter Love
Jeff Oloizia
John Cochran
Klancy Miller
Julia Moskin
Melissa Clark
Mary Celeste Beall
Brady Langmann
Adrienne Westenfeld
David Zilber
Bente Svendsen
Bo Bech
Becca Parrish
Sean Donnola
Signe Birck
Lærke Posselt
Evan Sung
Candice Peoples
Sara Bonisteel
Kim Severson
Santiago Lastra Rodriguez
Andre Baranowski
Dennis Beasley

Dody Chang
Nicole Miziolek
Joshua David Stein
Laura Wanamaker
Alexandra White
Marina D'Amore
Sofia Clarke
Hotel Sanders
Hotel D'Angleterre
Café Det Vide Hus
Villa Haugen in
    Leinesfjord, Norway
Norwegian Seafood
    Council
Marc Blazer
Ben Mervis
Peter Kreiner
Ben Liebmann
Anders Selmer
Mads Refslund
Roderick Sloan
Diana Henry
Howie Kahn
William Wolfslau
Aubrey Martinson
Killian Fox
Christopher Sjuve
Christine Johnston
Dyana Messina
Melissa Esner
Tim Duggan

Illustrations